Devotions Along The Oregon Trail

Jay and Sherrie Mennenga

Potential Press

Pocatello, Idaho

May this book enrich
your "journey."

Jay Mennenga

Devotions Along The Oregon Trail

ISBN Number: 0-9637732-2-4

Library of Congress Catalog Card Number: 97-75571

Acknowledgements

Cover picture courtesy of **Larry("Turbo") Stewart,** Milton, Iowa. Taken at Ft. Bridger, WY, 1997.

Material and maps about the Great Migration courtesy of Lloyd Coffman, **Blazing A Wagon Trail To Oregon: A Weekly Chronicle Of The Great Migration Of 1843,** Enterprise, OR, Echo Books, 1993.

Graphic design and layout by **R&L Publishing**, Rod& Linda Egli, Pocatello, ID

Printed by **Gilliland Printing**, Arkansas City, Kansas

All Scripture quotes taken from the New International Version of **The Living Insights Study Bible**, Grand Rapids, MI, Zondervan Publishing House, 1996.

DEDICATION

For all mothers from whom ideas,

depth, courage and birth honor our land;

especially to Marvieu Onalee

Mennenga and the late Helen Afton

Farrar Dewey for their tenderness

and strength along the

"Trail of Our Lives."

S.D.M.

INTRODUCTION

I have long matched my daily Bible reading times with wondering about the covered wagon path of the westward movement. As I slipped into a quiet time with the Lord, the oxen hoof beats, calico quilts and sunbonnet ladies would roll past my closed eyes.

It took me 30 years to realize those imaginative moments were an actual scriptural application of significance for me - a way to relive my interest in both the Oregon-California Trail adventures, and make come alive the daily faithful words of the Bible-**then and now**.

There was nothing to equal the migration on the Overland Trail over 150 years ago. Excitement, hope and imagination were running high. It takes only a slight shift in vision to look back and climb atop a trail rock, or give thanks for the safety and supplies of the rough journey.

The **format** of this book consists of three parts, **1843, Today and Lesson.** First, Jay has identified daily routines and challenges(such as river crossings) faced by the pioneers(**1843**). The excellent book **Blazing A Wagon Train To Oregon: A Weekly Chronicle of the Great Migration of 1843** by Lloyd W. Coffman, provides this historical background.

Second, these pioneer experiences become relevant by asking questions(**Today**). Third, a lesson on these topics is applied for the reader, using references from the New International Version of the Bible(**Lesson**). Related Passages deepen the journey.

Jay and I were married just two years ago, in 1995. Our home is only 11 miles from the Oregon Trail that passed through Ft. Hall, a major supply fort for the pioneers. We have our separate daily quiet times, seeking the Lord in the morning. Jay heads for a rose garden a few blocks away, and I settle down in an old chair near the kitchen. We rejoin replenished and refreshed - something many of the pioneers may have done.

Our lives and historical interests have miraculously intertwined with tourism, guests, beds to make, meals to serve and "mystery theatres" to present. Through all of these elements, we try to (1) daily touch base with what the Lord wants and (2) find the courage to carry out these activities. No doubt the pioneers also needed His strength and guidance for their journey.

Together we try to apply what perhaps could have been the settler's early morning whispered prayers, or exhausted evening vespers that long hard half-year on the Trail. I'm grateful for Jay's help, care, love and pioneer spirit on this journey together.

Sherrie Dewey Mennenga
Pocatello, Idaho
October 1997

Catching The "Fever": The Decision To Go To Oregon

There were many reasons why the pioneers decided to travel by wagon train to Oregon. This week's devotions deal with these motivations. Welcome aboard!

May 7

Economic Reasons

1843

The Panic of 1837 **depressed** prices for Midwestern farmers. They were working harder and making less, selling their crops under what it cost to produce. There was not a market for their crops and supply had outstripped demand. Some farmers began to look West for a possible answer to their economic **problems**.

Today

How do we react when facing economic problems today? Maybe we have lost a job. Maybe our investments in the stock market have tumbled. It's a bad year for our crops, due to blight and the weather. We face unexpected medical bills.

Lesson On Financial Challenges

The Apostle Paul affirms the promise of Jesus in **Philippians 4:19:** "And my God will **meet all your needs** according to his glorious riches in Christ Jesus." Here Jesus is promising to meet all our **needs**-not our wants- according to **His riches**-not our ideas. We have to be willing to trust Him for our financial welfare.

Related Passages: Matt 6:24-34; 1 Cor 16:1-4
1 Tim 6:3-10

May 8

Risk-Taking and Self-Concept

1843

What kind of person would give up the security of most of their possessions, leave their family and friends, and head 2,000 miles through unknown territory? They had to have a high degree of self-concept, willing to try new experiences. They had the **confidence** that their efforts would succeed, and they would arrive safely in Oregon.

Today

Are you a **risk-taker** today? Are you willing to move to an unknown state or country for a better job, or because you are "called by God" for a specific purpose? Do you have the confidence that your efforts will be rewarded in this new land? Or would you rather enjoy the status quo in a familiar environment, staying where you are?

Lesson On "Christ-Confidence"

From where does our self-concept come? From our family, friends, and environment. But also from God, who makes it positive! After all we are made in **His image**, as stated in Genesis 1:27, "So God created man in his own image, in the image of God he created him; male and female he created them." That's how important we are to God. How important is God to us?

Related Passages: Gen 12:1,4; Deut 31:5-6
Psalm 63

May 9

Restlessness and Contentment

1843

Ever since the 1804-06 Lewis and Clark expedition to explore the vast American territory in the West, Americans wondered what this land was like. Glowing reports came from Oregon promising "**fertile farmland**, and pigs running through the streets with the knives and forks already in them, ready to eat." Midwestern farmers, tired of their hard work on the farm for little or no profit, literally saw the grass being greener in Oregon. As Jesse Applegate stated, "the inherent restlessness of our nature" [1] caused some to find out more about this promised land. Maybe they should check it out for themselves.

Today

Have you heard that the "grass is greener" on the other side of the country, or in the next town or state? Have these reports, whether true or not, caused you to be dissatisfied with your present position? Can you consider a possible move while enjoying your current conditions? Have you looked beyond without fully appreciating today?

Lesson On Contentment

Isaiah sees the wicked "like the tossing sea, which cannot rest."(Isaiah 57:20) What is the antidote for restlessness? **Contentment.** The Apostle Paul gave us one answer in the Book of Phillipians(. . . "for I have learned to be content whatever the circumstances."Phil. 4: 11). Through the power of Christ, you can still enjoy your present environment while preparing for a move to another place.

Related Passages: Phil 4:12; 1 Tim 6:16
Heb 13:5

May 10

Adventure Of A New Situation

1843

Some of the pioneers venturing to Oregon saw it just like that- a great **adventure**. This was a chance to experience the frontier, to see Indians and new scenery, and to camp and meet new people along the way. Life was to be lived to the fullest. These people, especially the men, were convinced the journey was more important than the actual destination. They "smelled the sagebrush along the way." Life was exciting for these optimists.

Today

Do you have a zest for life, wanting to take in everything? You may like to travel, to meet new people, to take advantage of every opportunity and to partake in many cultural opportunities. Life is good for you. But the good can get in the way of the best. How can you move from the "**good life**" to the "**best life**?"

Lesson On Conforming To His Will

Jesus had this to say about making life the **best** it can be for you: ". . . I have come that they may have life, and have it to the full."(John 10:10) He wants us to have an abundant life that can best be lived by first finding, and then doing His will for our life. Life can more **fully** be enjoyed through Him.

Related Passages: Psalm 40:8; 143:10
Rom 12:2; Col 2:16

May 11

Seeking A Healthier Climate

1843

The lush farmlands of the Mississippi River Valley yielded plentiful crops- and also mosquitoes. Unbeknown to these farmers, these pesky critters carried the dreaded disease ague, a form of **malaria.** The Midwestern winters were also severe, with their blizzards and bitterly cold climate. Thus sickness was prevalent to these settlers both in the hot humid summers and the long cold winters. No wonder they saw Oregon, with its temperate climate, yet green fertile farmland, as their paradise. One more reason to load up and head West in their wagons.

Today

Do you live in an area of the country where the **climate** affects your health? It could be the pollen and dust affecting your breathing, if you are an asthmatic. The cold winters may trigger arthritis. You may even get frequent colds. Living in a cloudy rainy environment can even affect your disposition, making you SAD with Seasonal Affective Disorder. Should you move to a healthier climate, or stay where you are and deal with your sicknesses?

Lesson On Healing

Jesus is the Great Physician. The Gospels recount many instances of His healing the following persons: an official's son(John 4:46-54); Peter's mother-in-law(Matthew 8:14-15); and a man born blind(John 9:1-41) Jesus even raised Jairus's daughter to life(Mark 5:21-43) and raised Lazarus from the dead.(John 11:1-44) These same miracles can happen today, through **Christ's healing power.**

Related Passages: Matt 4:23; 9:35; James 5:14-15
Prov 16:24

May 12

Mission and Vision: Manifest Destiny

1843

Some of the pioneers who went to Oregon had a vision greater than their own welfare. They called it "**Manifest Destiny**." They thought it was their "manifest destiny to overspread and possess as the whole of the continent which Providence has given us for the great experiment of liberty and federated self-government."[2] Their motives were more altruistic and patriotic than simply claiming free land for their families. They were on a **mission** to Oregon, to help claim this land for the United States.

Today

Most of the time we are concerned with the details of living: working at our jobs, providing for our families, enjoying our friends, and planning leisure activities. We may also be involved in our church or communities on a volunteer basis. Occasionally, during national or international events, such as wars or natural disasters, we look beyond ourselves to help our country or neighbors in need. Our **vision** then extends beyond our parochial boundaries. How can we keep this vision of the greater good alive?

Lesson On Vision

For a meaningful life we need to believe in a cause **greater** than ourselves. For Christians, the cause is Christ. Paul's life was evidence of his mission as he summarized, "For to me, to live is Christ and to die is gain."(Philippians 1:21) Even Jesus stated His purpose on earth as greater than himself: "For I have come down from heaven not to do my will but to do the will of Him who sent me."(John 6:38)

Related Passages: Isaiah 1:28; 60:12; Dan 9
Phil 2:4

May 13

A New Start

1843

Some of the pioneers who went to Oregon simply wanted a **new start**. Their parents may have died, and they had no more responsbilities to care for them. They may have had personal problems with their marriages and families falling apart. A few may have committed crimes such as assault or robbery, and hadn't yet been caught. The frontier offered a place to **hide** from their past lives.

Today

Do you wish you could make a new start? Maybe you have just experienced a business failure, a divorce or death of your parents. Or your children have "left the nest" and you are free to move to a new location. On a personal note, do you make New Year's resolutions, only to not keep them? How can you start keeping those **resolutions**?

Lesson On Old And New Life In Christ

We can "grit our teeth" and try to be a better person. But in our own strength, sooner or later we will eventually encounter a crisis with which we cannot cope. We need to tap into a **power** greater than ourselves, one that can change our desires from the inside out. Jesus furnishes us this power if we ask Him to come in and substitue His desires for our selfish attitudes and actions. "Therefore if any one is in Christ, he is a **new creation**; the old has gone, the new has come." (II Corinthians 5:17)

Related Passages: Is 62:2; Jer 31:31
Luke 22:20; Col 3:1-14

Preparing To Go: Knowing What Supplies To Take

The pioneers had to choose their supplies carefully for their 2,000 mile trek to Oregon.

May 14

Wagons and Tents

1843

Covered wagons were actually small **farm wagons**-ten feet long, four feet wide, with sides 2 1/2 feet high, capable of carrying 2,500 pounds of supplies. The wagon had to be both strong and light. A canvas top provided some protection from the elements, and a modicum of privacy. The running gear, including the **wheels**, was the most important part of the wagon. Since there was no room in the wagons, the pioneers slept in tents.

Today

Have you ever moved your household goods yourself? Then you have faced the challenge of loading, and trying to find a **space** for everything. Have you camped in a tent, where you moved every day? Then you can identify with the transient feeling the pioneers faced on the Trail.

Lesson On Contentment While Traveling

As Christians we can be assured that our life on earth is not our **permanent home**. We're here to (1) find out what God wants us to do and then to (2) accomplish His will in our lives. Jesus ascended into heaven to prepare a place for us, as He promised in John 14: 2,3. Then He will come back for us. Are you ready for His return?

Related Passages: Isaiah 54: 2; 2 Cor 5:1-4
2 Pet 1:13

May 15

Which Supplies To Take: Food

1843

The pioneers, with no refrigeration, took food items that would not spoil on the 22 week journey. The following were **recommended amounts** for each adult: 150 pounds of flour or hard bread; 25 pounds of bacon or pork; 15 pounds of coffee; 25 pounds of sugar, and seasonings such as salt and pepper. **3** In addition they took cattle, goats and chickens for milk, butter and eggs. On the plains buffalo would provide meat and the rivers would supply fish. The diet was basic but monotonous.

Today

Today, how do you determine which types of **food** to buy? Do you purchase only those items that are nutritious, or the junk foods with empty calories? Do you purchase brand names, store brands, or generic items? Or do you buy items by the type of packaging and not the contents? Or are you self-sufficient, growing some of your own food in a garden?

Lesson On The Bread Of Life

The Bible has a lot to say about the importance of **food**, particularly bread in both a literal and a figurative sense. Jesus, when teaching the disciples to pray, included the phrase, "Give us this day our **daily bread**."(Luke 11:3) Jesus, when tempted by the devil, declared in Luke 4: 4, "Man does not live by bread alone, but by every word that comes from the mouth of God." Jesus is placing the Bible as more important than our daily bread.

Related Passages: Deut 8:3; Prov 30:8
John 6:35-51

May 16

Which Supplies To Take: Livestock

1843

The pioneers tried to be as **self-sufficient** as possible when traveling. Since most of them were farmers, it was only logical to take some of their livestock. Cattle furnished milk, and meat if needed. Goats provided cheese and butter, while chickens laid eggs. Jesse Applegate referred to this long motley line of wagons and livestock in his writings, "A Day With The Cow Column of 1843." These animals were a more reliable source of food than finding buffalo or catching fish along the way.

Today

Do you try to be self-sufficient in today's modern technological world? Do you **store** extra food and supplies in your home in case of a natural disaster or power failure? What if there was a trucker's strike, or riot that closed grocery stores? Would you be able to survive in the city? If you live on a farm, would you be able to use your own crops and livestock to survive?

Lesson On Caring For Our Needs

The Psalms contain promises that the Lord will provide food for our **physical needs**. He will give food to the hungry.(Psalm 146:7) David observes,"I was young and now I am old, yet I have never seen the righteous forsaken or their children begging for bread."(Psalm 37:25). He owns "the cattle on a thousand hills."(Psalm 50:10)

Related Passages: 1 Sam 6:7; Psalm 144:3
1 Pet 5:2-7

May 17

Which Supplies To Take: Miscellaneous Goods

1843

The emigrants took as many **supplies** as they could, even if they were not directly related to providing for their basic needs. Some of these were "clothes, cooking utensils, tools for repairing the road and wagons, chains and ropes for the animals and wagons, groundcloths to prevent moisture from getting under tents at night, firearms for hunting and protection from the Indians and robbers, medicines, religious books-including a Bible- and a fiddle for singing and relaxing at night." **4**

Today

When you are going on a trip, what supplies do you take? Do you take only the **necessities**(food, different types of clothes, toiletries, tools, etc.), or do you provide for your intellectual, spiritual and aesthetic needs by taking books, compact discs or tapes, and a camera? Do you take your **Bible** with you, for your daily devotions or sharing with others?

Lesson On Studying The Word Of God

The **Bible** is a unique book, because you first have to know the author personally before you can understand its content. When you invite Jesus Christ into your life, reading the Bible becomes more exciting and meaningful to you. You will eventually be able to agree with the writer of Hebrews that "the Word of God is living and active. Sharper than any double-edged sword, it **penetrates** even to dividing the soul and spirit, joints and marrow; it judges the thoughts and attitudes of the heart."(4:12)

Related Passages: Ezekiel 7:10; Matt 10:24
John 5:39; 1 Tim 2:15

May 18

Long Term Versus Short Term Goods

1843

The pioneers also took supplies needed for settling in Oregon, once they arrived. "Among them were farming implements, tools for building houses and household furniture." **5** Thus they had to **balance** taking the short-term supplies necessary for the journey with those that would be used on a long-term basis. Should they take the keepsake items such as china cabinets or lace doilies? What about taking a cast-iron cooking stove or wrought-iron bed?

Today

How do you balance your **short-term** with your **long-term** goals today? Do you buy something on credit now, or save to purchase it later? Do you set aside part of your current expenditures for your retirement? Do you mainly concern yourself with the things of this world, or do you think in terms of eternity?

Lesson On Planning For Eternity

Paul gives us this advice on where we should focus: "So we fix our eyes not on what is seen, but on what is **unseen.** For what is seen is temporary, but what is unseen is **eternal**."(2 Corinthians 4:18)

Jesus says our treasures should be in heaven: "Do not store up for yourself treasures on earth, where moth and rust destory, and where thieves break in and steal. But store up for yourselves **treasures** in heaven, where moth and rust do not destroy. For where your treasure is, there your **heart** will be also."(Matthew 6: 19-21).

Related Passages: Eccl 3:11; Matt 6:28-34
Phil 3

May 19

Loading The Wagons

1843

Once the pioneers decided what supplies to take to Oregon, they had to decide how to **load** them into the wagon. The most accessible goods (food, clothing and firearms) needed to be near the top and the sides of the wagons. Those goods (tools for farming and building) that were not needed until their arrival in Oregon could be placed at the bottom. The bulky furniture had to be placed in the middle, leaving little room to ride or lie down. Anything over 2,500 pounds was considered too heavy a load for the animals to pull, and should be left behind.

Today

Do you face **heavy loads** in your life? Maybe it is not physical loads like the pioneers had, but emotional burdens from your family needing attention, or your friends needing advice. Maybe you are facing a financial load, with the bills piling up. Are you facing burnout in your job? How do you face these burdens when you are at your wits end?

Lessons On Burden-Bearing

Jesus will bear our burdens if we will ask for his assistance. David praised the Lord . . . "who daily **bears our burdens.**"(Psalm 68:19) Jesus promises rest for the weary in Matthew 11: 28 with his command, "Come to me, all you who are weary and burdened, and I will give you rest." We can do our work in combination with his outside heavenly assistance. Try it and see!

Related Passages:: Matt 11:28-30; Luke 9:23-27
Gal 6:2-5

May 20

Rules For The Journey

1843

With the supplies chosen and loaded on the wagons, there remained an organizational item to be addressed. With 120 wagons and approximately 1,000 persons involved in this migration, **rules** had to be drawn up. Consequently a written document with the purpose "of keeping good order and promoting civil and military discipline" was approved. **6** It was a democratic document, but only adult males could vote on the company affairs.

Today

We understand that rules are necessary to keep **order** in a civilized society. In our democratic society, we elect officials to make the laws and appoint officials to administer them. We have an aversion to authoritarian rule, since history has shown there are few benevolent dictators who don't abuse their power. How can we be assured that the rules we live by are for our benefit, and are just?

Lesson On Rules

God is the ultimate **law-giver**. He gave Moses the **Ten Commandments** as recorded in Exodus 20: 3-17. They still serve as a guide for an orderly society, especially the prohibitions against murder, stealing and lying. Jesus supplemented these commandments with the Golden Rule: "So in everything, do to others what you would have them do to you, for this sums up the Law and the Prophets."(Matthew 7: 12). These rules are excellent guides for our corporate lives today.

Related Passages: Lev 25:18; 2 Chron 7:12-18
Josh 1:7-9

Week One: May 21-May 27

The Journey Begins

This journey started the largest voluntary mass **migration** in human history. In the next 23 years over 350,000 persons would travel the Mormon, Oregon and California Trails.

May 21

Saying Goodbye To The Past

1843

Before the pioneers boarded their wagons, hugs were given to their families-children to their parents, aunts and uncles and grandparents. Longtime friends said their last farewells to each other. The mutual understanding was that once the families headed West, they would **never** see their homeland and loved ones again.

Today

Have you said **goodbye** to your family and friends, knowing it was the last time you would see them? What kind of emotions were you experiencing during this sentimental time? But you pushed on toward your goal, whether a better job or better environment for your family. How did you break the emotional ties of home?

Lesson On Forgetting The Past

Here is Paul's remedy for looking ahead, instead of back, as did Lot's wife(Genesis 19:26): "Forgetting what is **behind** and straining toward what is **ahead**, I press on toward the goal to win the prize for which God has called me heavenward in Christ Jesus."(Phil 3: 13-14) It's a matter of letting Christ refocus you from your past to the present.

Related Passages: Ex 12:31-42; Ps 1:1-3
Luke 5:19

May 22

The Excitement Of A New Beginning

1843

There was undoubtedly much **excitement** and enthusiam as the 120 wagons left Independence, Missouri, bound for Oregon. Even though they had the entire Trail ahead of them, the journey was invigorating-at least for awhile. A welcome change of pace from the routine of farm life. But for how long could they keep up this excitement? Maybe until the first disagreement or crisis developed.

Today

Do you start projects strong, only to find your enthusiasm waning as you get farther down the road? Are you a sprinter or a marthon runner? Do you have a "kick" at the end, or do you fade quickly, or don't finish at all? How can you possess the **stamina** to complete your project with excitement, finishing as strong as you start?

Lesson On Beginnings

Jesus promised that we would both start and finish our spiritual lives with Him: ". . . being confident of this, that He who began a good work in you will carry it on to completion until the day of Christ Jesus."(Phil 1: 6) When we first asked Christ into our lives, we were excited that our desires and interests changed. We wanted to read the Bible and tell others about Him. But then we had our "valleys" to go through after this peak experience. Jesus promises to be with us both on the mountaintops and in the valleys, until we meet Him in heaven.

Related Passages: Ex 3:7-10; Lev 25:38
John 1:1

May 23

Facing The Unknown

1843

At the same time the pioneers were excited, they were also **frightened.** They had a natural fear of the unknown. What lay ahead of them during the 1,932 miles to Oregon? They had heard stories of savage Indians waiting to attack them for their goods and possibly their scalps. Death and disease along the Trail were distinct possibilities. Still they took the risk and challenge to start out on their journey.

Today

How do you react when facing the unknown, be it a new business or job, a move to a new city, or meeting new neighbors? Are you energized or apprehensive by the unfamiliar territory you are in? Do you try to obtain as much information about your new situations beforehand, or move forward even though you don't know everything? How important is **faith** to your journey?

Lesson On Faith

". . . faith is being sure of what we **hope** for and certain of what we do not see."(Hebrews 11:1) If we had everything figured out beforehand, there would be no need for faith. Faith gives us the assurance that by trusting Christ for the outcome, His will be done in our lives. "We live by faith, not by sight."(II Corinthians 5: 7) We use faith in our everyday lives (turning on the lights and assuming they will work). How much more important to have faith in God to direct our lives.

Related Passages: Ps 37:23-24; Prov 16:9
1 Pet 2:20-22

May 24

A Guide For The Journey

1843

Hiring a **guide** was essential, since no one knew the way to Oregon, and there were no reliable maps to assist them. These emigrants choose a veteran Rocky Mountain fur trapper, John Gantt, to lead them. Jesse Applegate described him as, " a borderer who has passed his life on the verge of civilization and has been chosen to the post of leader from his knowledge of the savage and his experience in travel through roadless wastes." **7**

Today

When planning a trip, how do you know which travel guide to select? There's AAA, Frommer's and Mobil, to name a few. You might consider the following criteria: objectivity, reliability, degree of respect, thoroughness, and popularity. For your trip through life, do you use a **guide** and **guidebook**?

Lesson On Guides and Guidebooks

As Christians our guidebook is the **Bible**, since it "is God-breathed and is useful for teaching, rebuking, correcting and training in righteousness, so that the man of God may be thoroughly equipped for every good work."(II Timothy 3: 16-17) Even though truth exists apart from the teaching of the Scriptures, the Bible contains **all truth**. Thus it serves as a reliable guide for our lives. Jesus, the author of the Bible, therefore becomes our ultimate guide, even to the end(Psalm 48:14). "He guides me in the paths of righteousness for his name's sake."(Psalm 23:3)

Related Passages: Ex 13:20-21; Josh 24:26-28
Prov 3:5-6

May 25

"The Worst Traits Of Human Nature"

1843

The emigrants in this wagon train were fiercely **individualistic,** "in a new and trying position," with ten thousand little vexations continually recurring," stated Peter Burnett, that often brought out "the worse traits of human nature." **8** For example, wagons would jockey for position, so as to not be eating another's dust. They would seize an advantage for themselves without considering any courtesy for their fellow travelers.

Today

Do you try to seize the **advantage** in a particular situation? When driving, do you cut too closely in front of someone else in traffic to get to your destination quicker? Do you think only in terms of what you want (selfishness), or do you consider the welfare of others?

Lesson On Thinking Of Others

Paul contrasts a person's sinful nature with one **empowered** by the Holy Spirit: "Do not be deceived: God cannot be mocked. A man reaps what he sows. The one who sows to please his sinful nature, from that nature will reap destruction; the one who sows to please the Spirit, from the Spirit will reap eternal life."(Galations 6: 7-8) Paul also admonishes us to ". . . look not only to your own interests, but also to the interests of others."(Philippians 2: 4). These are good reminders for the pioneers, and ourselves as well.

Related Passages: Psalm 32:5-11; Prov 20:4-9
Rom 8:1-11

May 26

Crossing The Kansas River

1843

On this day the **Oregon Emigrating Company**(the name the pioneers choose for their wagon train) faced their first major obstacle-the crossing of the Kansas River. Since the spring had been rainy, the river was swollen. Fording was not a possibility, so a log ferry was built for the wagons. After several near drownings, everyone crossed safely. But the danger of river crossings became a reality, a fact they would have to consider the rest of the trip.

Today

Are there certain things you **fear** in your life? Maybe its the fear of heights, of falling, or being in the water? Maybe you feel overwhelmed by circumstances in your job or family. Events and people are closing in on you, making you feel uncomfortable. What can you do to prevent this "drowning" feeling of being overwhelmed?

Lesson On Not Feeling Overwhelmed

The Scriptures offer several promises to prevent us from being **overwhelmed** by the "waters of life." "When you pass through the waters, I will be with you; and when you pass through the rivers, they will not sweep over you."(Isaiah 43: 2) David praises the Lord because, "He lifted me out of the slimy pit, out of the mud and mire; he set my feet on a rock and gave me a firm place to stand."(Psalm 40: 2) Jesus can do the same for you if you can see Him **above** your circumstances.

Related Passages: Ezek 47:1-6; John 7:37-39
Rev 22:1-5

May 27

Remember The Sabbath

NOTE: I am assuming the 1843 pioneers rested every Sunday, after traveling 6 days. Therefore the devotion every 7 days will relate to the **"Sabbath Rest."** Also you will see a map on these "Sabbath pages", using dots to delineate their weekly progress. **9** There were twenty-two Sundays on the journey.

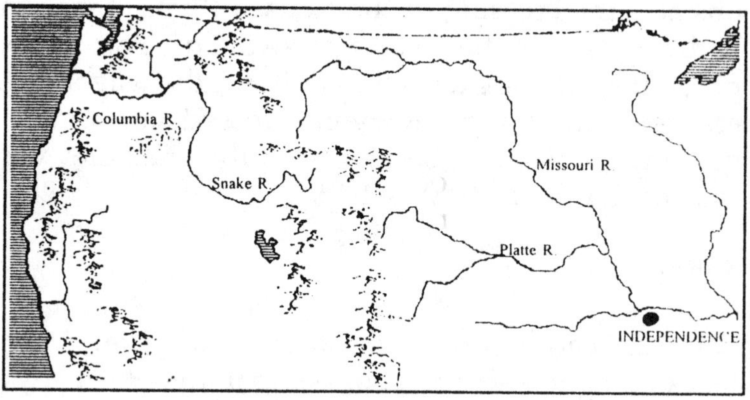

1843

The first week the Company traveled 55 miles from their starting point at Elm Grove(16 miles west of Independence, Missouri)(see above map) It took them six exhaustive days to cross the Kansas River. Now it was time to rest and refresh themselves.

Today

Do you take time to rest after working six days during the week? God set a precedent for us to set aside one day in seven to rest. "And God blessed the seventh day and made it holy, because on it He rested from all the work of creating that He had done."(Genesis 2: 3).

Related Passages: Ex 23:10-13; Psalm 37:7-9
Matt 11:25-30

Week Two: May 28-June 3

The Moving Community

Since it took six days to cross the Kansas River, the pioneers realized how delays could affect their eventual arrival date in Oregon. Therefore they had to keep moving, possibly making up time.

May 28

Election Of Wagonmaster

1843

The emigrants did not elect a permanent wagonmaster until they crossed the Kansas River. In this way they could observe which **candidates** were suitable for this important job. Their election procedure consisted of the voters(adult males) chasing the candidates across the prairie, and forming a line behind their favorite one. The candidate with the longest "tail" was the winner. This was really "running for office". **10**

Today

Instead of the old wagonmaster procedure, we choose our leaders by secret ballot. We expect our leaders to be competent and qualified for the position for which they are running. If we don't like them, we can vote them out of office. Not much job security. What about our **security** in this world?

Lesson On Elections And Choosing

As "born-again" Christians, we have the security of knowing God has chosen us, "before the creation of the world to be holy and blameless in His sight."(Ephesians 1:4) Thus our security is **in Christ**, not in man-made institutions.

Related Passages:: Deut 7:6-11; Psalm 89:1-4
Prov 22: 1,29; 1 Cor 1:10

May 29

Yoked Oxen

1843

Most wagons used oxen for their locomotion, since they were durable and easily managed. Three pair of **yoked oxen** were the preferred number. The yoke was "a heavy bar of wood about four feet long that contained two U-shaped, round hickory bows." **10** Once the oxen's heads were inside the bows, pins at the top of the bar secured them. Then when the oxen moved, they would push against the bar together, providing pulling power.

Today

Do you **"pull together"** in your relationships with others? It could be a business partner, your spouse or your family members. What if one person wants to "stop" and you want to "go", or vice versa? How do you handle this possible disparity? Can all parties involved in a particular issue "pull" together for the sake of a common goal?

Lesson On Being Yoked Together

The Bible contains a prohibition against Christians entering into serious agreements with non-Christians, whether in business or marriage. "Do not be yoked together with unbelievers. For what do righteousness and wickedness have in common? Or what fellowship can light have with darkness?"(2 Corinthians 6:14) The Bible also contains **promises** to uphold those who are struggling under a heavy load. David writes, "The Lord upholds all who fall and lifts up all who are bowed down."(Psalm 145:14) He lightens our load!

Related Passages: Deut25:4; 1 Sam 6:6-9
Is 1:2-3

May 30

Importance of Grass

1843

The availability of good grass was the most important factor in determining when the wagon train started on their journey. The pioneers waited until the grass was four inches high, providing adequate food for the oxen. Bernard Reid called **grass**, along with **wood** and **water**, "the emigrant's trinity of good things." **11** Because of the wetter climate east of the 100th Meridian, grass was available more during the first part of the journey than later on in the Western arid desert.

Today

Grass is the sign of new life and **renewal**, especially in the Spring, with its budding flowers and blossoming trees. Everything seems fresh during this time of the year as God renews his creation. **Grass** also symbolizes rest and relaxing. Do you look for times of rest, renewal and relaxation in the midst of your hectic schedule?

Lesson On Refreshing and Rootedness

David paints an idyllic picture of refreshing in the well-known 23rd Psalm: "He makes me lie down in green pastures, He leads me beside quiet waters, He restores my soul."(vv. 2-3). Just as grass needs **roots** to grow, so do we who have received Christ Jesus. Paul encourages us to ". . . continue to live in Him, rooted and built up in him, strenghtened in the faith as you were taught, and overflowing with thankfulness."(Colossions 2:6-7). Thus refreshing can lead to a deeper walk with Christ. Try it!

Related Passages: Gen 1:11-13; Ps 72:16-19
Matt 6:25-28

May 31

Walking

1843

Contrary to the Hollywood movies showing families riding in the wagons, almost everyone **walked** the 1,932 miles to Oregon. There were four reasons for this: (1) there was little room to ride, since the wagons were loaded with supplies; (2) the ride was very bumpy(no shock absorbers!); (3) the emigrants didn't want to add additional weight for the oxen to pull; and (4) walking afforded time to socialize with acquaintances and friends along the Trail.

Today

How important is walking to you? Can you walk to work? Do you enjoying walking for exercise and to relieve stress? Can you think, pray and receive insights while walking? Or do you walk with others, sharing your thoughts and ideas? Do you think you could have walked the entire way to Oregon in 22 weeks? How many pairs of shoes would you wear out? How's your **spiritual walk**?

Lesson On Our Spiritual Walk

Do you have a consistent daily **quiet time** with God, talking with him in prayer, listening to his guidance and reading His Word? Psalm 84 contains a promise for "those whose walk is blameless: no good thing does He withhold."(v.11) Joshua admonishes the Israelites . . ."to love the Lord your God, to **walk** in all His ways, to obey His commands, to hold fast to Him and to serve Him with all your heart and all your soul."(22:5)

Related Passages: Is 40:29-31; 2 Cor 5:6-8;
John 1:5-8

June 1

Stealing

1843

The biggest fear the emigrants had from the **Indians** was not being attacked and scalped. It was the stealing of their horses. The Indians turned this type of stealing into an art form, to the point of stealing a horse, even though a pioneer had the rope wrapped around his arm at night! To the Indians this thievery was justified. "It represented a way of collecting toll for the use of their land." **12** Sometimes stealing was done by "white Indians"(whites dressed like Indians to cast the blame on them).

Today

Do you think **stealing** is ever justified? Should you steal to supply food for your family? Do you steal your employer's time at work and supplies for personal use? What about claiming deductions that are not really yours on your income tax? Do you tithe at your church?

Lesson On Stealing

Stealing is prohibited by one of the Ten Commandments. (Exodus 20:15) Jesus reinforces this commandment in the New Testament when advising the rich young ruler in Matthew 19:18. We can **rob God** by not giving our whole tithe to him.(Malachi 3: 8-10) Paul warns those who have been stealing to not steal anymore, "but (they) must work, doing something useful with his own hands, that he may have something to share with those in need."(Ephesians 4:28) Good advice for us.

Related Passages: Mal 3:8-12; John 10:1-6
Phil 2:5-11

June 2

Delivering Letters

1843

Writing letters was the only way the emigrants had to communicate with their friends and families back in civilization. The problem was how to deliver these **letters** in the pre-Pony Express era. The pioneers used the only means available, fur trappers going East to sell their goods. M.M. McCarver writes, "The return of a company of mountain traders to the settlements presents an opportunity for writing which I feel much inclined to embrace." **13** Thus perfect strangers carried their mail. Many letters and diaries remain today.

Today

In today's technological age we have several choices to transmit the written word-by e-mail, fax or the traditional "snail mail." What's more important to you, the **speed** of the delivery or the **quality** of the letter? How credible is the person or machine delivering the letter?

Lesson On Letters

The Apostle Paul adds a human dimension to his second letter to the Corinthians with this conclusion: "You yourselves are our **letter**, written on our hearts, known and read by everybody. You show that you are a letter from Christ, the result of our ministry, written not with ink but with the Spirit of the living God, not on tablets of stone but on tablets of human hearts."(3:2-3) A strong witness to someone else is our life, lived through the power of the Holy Spirit.

Related Passages: 2 Sam 11:14-17; John 7:10-19
Rom 2:25-29

June 3

Reflecting On The Sabbath

1843

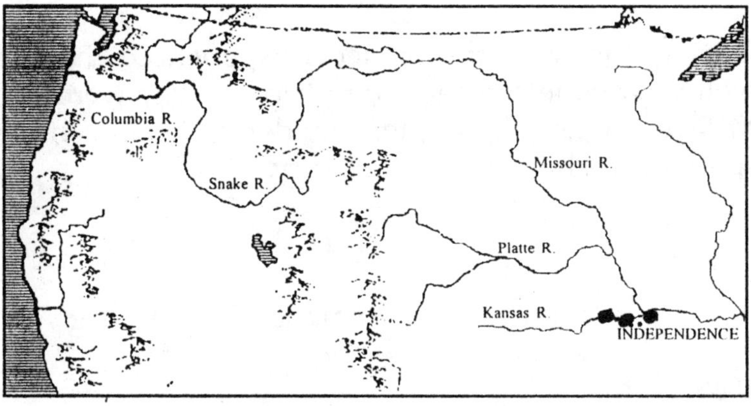

The Oregon Emigrating Company was now heading northwest to the West Fork of the Blue River. They had tried to make up for the six days it took to cross the Kansas River. But is was now time to **rest** and reflect on the previous week.

Today

Do you take time once a week to **reflect** on the following questions:

"What does my work mean?
For whom did I do this work?
How well was this work done?
Why did I do this(work?)
What results did I expect?
What(results) did I receive?" **14**

Lesson On Reflection

As we draw closer to God we ". . . reflect the Lord's glory, (and) are being transformed into His likeness with ever-increasing glory, which comes from the Lord, who is the Spirit."(2 Corintians 3:18)

Related Passages: Gal 6:1-5; 1 Pet 1:13-21
Rev 22:12-17

Week Three: Stormy Weather

June 4-10

During this week the pioneers experienced the worst and wettest **weather** on the entire trip. They were still in the Midwest, where lightning, thunder and rain combine for a spectacular show of Nature's fury.

June 4

Facing The Storms: Lightning

1843

Pierson Reading provided this description of **lightning** on the plains: "The whole atmosphere seemed charged with electric fluid, and during some five hours seemed a continuous blaze." **15** The biggest problem was that a near strike would cause the oxen to stampede, overturning the wagons. One horse was killed by lightning. **16**

Today

Does lightning **awe** you or **frighten** you? Do you think of the power the Creator displays in putting on this light show for us?

Lesson On Heavenly Lightning

Lightning is used in the Bible to get our **attention.** Lightning accompanied the giving of the 10 Commandments to the Israelites(Exodus 20:18). Jesus will return to earth "as lightning that comes from the east is visible even in the west"(Matthew 24:27) Are you ready for His soon return?

Related Passages: Ps 135:5-7; Dan 10:4-9
Matt 24:23-25

June 5

Facing The Storms: Thunder

1843

Even though lightning was more dangerous during storms, it was the **thunder** that reverberated across the open prairie. Overton Johnson called the thunder claps "a constant roar" with some peals resembling "the discharge of volleys of artillery." **17** The pioneers had not experienced storms this loud on their Midwestern farms.

Today

Does thunder amaze you or frighten you? Do you think of the power the **Creator** displays in putting on this incredible sound show for you? How can we experience some of this enormous power in our lives?

Lesson On Thunder

Thunder is seen in the Bible as exhibiting God's **glory** and **power:** ". . . the God of glory thunders, the Lord thunders over the mighty waters."(Psalm 29:3) God is seen as "Mightier than the thunder of the great waters . . ."(Psalm 93:4) In the Book of Job God's voice is described as one that "thunders in marvelous ways; He does great things beyond our understanding."(37:5) When God is handing out judgments during the Tribulation period of history, His voice sounds like seven thunders.(Revelation 10:3). Surely we need to heed His voice when He speaks to us about our lives, **commands** us to do something or **prohibits** us from a particular type of action. He has the force of the skies behind His voice.

Related Passages: 2 Sam 22:14-16; Mark 3:13-17
Rev 19: 6-8

June 6

Facing The Storms: Torrential Rains

1843

The **rains** that accompanied the lightning and thunder were **torrential** in nature, flooding the campsites and getting everything wet, including provisions, bedding and clothing. Sara Hill describes this disheartening scene: "it even floated ox yokes. Where we crossed(the Blue River) the evening before the next morning it was forty feet deep." **18** Sleeping in wet clothing was not being happy campers.

Today

Rain can either be gentle and refreshing, or it comes in torrential downpours. We need it in moderate and regular **intervals**, otherwise we experience either droughts or floods. In our Christian walk, are we refreshed by the "waters of life", or do we go through desert experiences, where our spiritual life is dry. Maybe we participate in too many church activities, flooding our soul. How can we strike a **balance** between feast or famine in our relationship with Christ?

Lesson On Rain

We need to establish a daily quiet time, spending time meditating on God's goodness. Then God's mercy will fall on us like a "**sweet spring rain.**" **19** If we cultivate this holy habit, we will not be overwhelmed by the "waters of affliction."(Isaiah 30:20) Being too "wet" spiritually can be as dangerous as being too "dry." Regular doses of His word is the key to a balanced Christian life. Try it.

Related Passages: Gen 7:1-6; Eccl 11:1-4
Matt 5:43-48

June 7

Women Going On The Trail

1843

Women did not have much input in the decision to travel to Oregon. "Not one wife initiated the idea; it was always the husband." Another historian concluded, "the period of the Overland Trail migration produces overwhelming evidence that **women** did not greet the idea of going West with enthusiasm." **20** But they went West anyway.

Today

How do husbands and wives make important **decisions** today, like moving? Do you list the pros and cons? Do you pray, seeking God's guidance? Do you decide by consensus or by voting? If children are involved, can they also vote? Does the husband make the final decision, after considering input from all?

Lesson On Family Decision-Making

Ephesians 5: 22-33 contains guidelines on the roles of the husbands and wives. Wives are supposed to **submit** to the husbands "as to the Lord."(v 22) At the same time husbands are supposed to **love** their wives "as Christ loved the church and gave Himself up for her."(v 25) The husband "must love his wife as he loves himself, and the wife must respect her husband."(v 33) If each spouse is looking out for the interests of the other, as Christ looks out for His church, decisions will be made that are according to His will.

Related Passages: Ps 101:2; Eph 4:31-32
1 Pet 3:1-7

June 8

New births On The Trail

1843

The **birth** of children couldn't be delayed just because the women were walking the Trail. Several women were pregnant when the Company left Missouri in May. No doubt others became pregnant on the Trail. Jesse Looney wrote in October, 1843, "there were some eight to ten births" on the Trail. **21** Life goes on, Trail or no Trail.

Today

The birth of a child is one of the most important **miracles** a married couple can experience. Everyone who sees the child shares in this excitement of the new birth. No matter how the baby really looks, he or she is beautiful. How important are new births and beginnings to you?

Lesson On New Births

Jesus compares the **physical birth** of a child with **spiritual birth** in John 3: "I tell you the truth, no one can see the kingdom of God unless he is born again. . . no one can enter the kingdom of God unless he is born of water and the Spirit."(vv 3,5) Jesus is saying that everyone who inherits eternal life must first be "born again" by asking Christ to personally come into their life. This is a miracle from above more important than childbirth. Have you become "**born-again**," becoming a Child of God and inheriting eternal life?

Related Passages: John 3; I Cor 15:1-4
Eph 2: 8-9

June 9

Smaller Units Work Best

1843

The Company, composed of 120 wagons, divided over the issue of caring for **cattle**. "Those with more than ten head of loose stock went one way, those with less went the other." The "Cow Column," headed by Jesse Applegate, further divided his 60 wagons into 15 platoons of 4 each. This division of labor showed the importance of smaller units functioning more efficiently. **22**

Today

Are you frustrated by the bureaucracy, whether it be government, the military, the school system, big business, or even your church? Do you enjoy negotiating the maze of "phone mail jail," never talking to a live employee? How can you find **meaningful relationships** in today's society?

Lesson On Relationships

The key to building relationships is through the creation of **small groups** in your church. In a small group Bible study of 8-12, participants can share their lives and prayer requests while studying the Scriptures. This is Paul's model: ". . . the things you have heard me say in the presence of many witnesses entrust to reliable men who will also be qualified to teach others."(2 Timothy 2:2). Join or start a small relational study group at your church.

Related Passages: Prov 22:17; Heb 10:24-25
James 1: 24-25

June 10

Assembling On The Sabbath

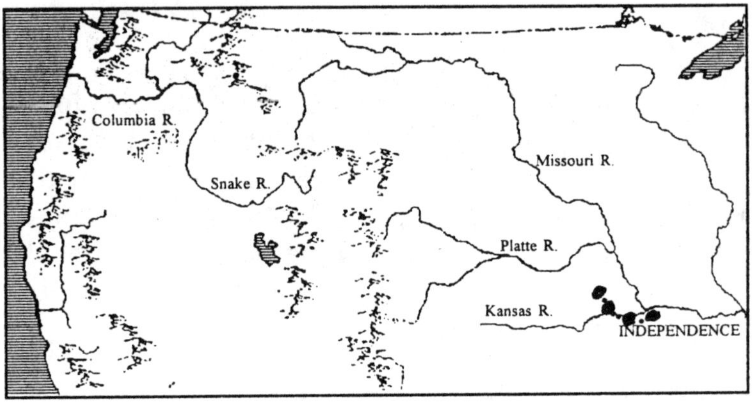

1843

This was a wet week for the Company. They were between two major rivers, the Kansas and the Platte, continuing their northwest trek. Time to rest and dry out from the storms.

Today

What do you do on Sundays after a hectic week? Would you rather "sleep in" than go to church? "It's the only day I have to snooze and catch up on my shopping and house/yard work," you explain. "I'll watch a sermon on TV." Or do you regularly attend church, looking forward to a time of praise, instruction and fellowhip? What does the Bible say about regular church attendance? "Let us not give up meeting together, as some are in the habit of doing, but let us encourage one another-and all the more as we see the Day approaching."(Hebrews 10:25) Find a Bible believing church, and attend regularly, or continue to regularly support your church.

Related Passages: Prov 30:5; Is 55:10-11
Heb 4:12

Indian Territory

June 11

Dealing With Different Races

The Company was now passing through territory designated for the **Indians**. In 1830 the Indian Removal Bill was passed, swapping Indian lands in the East for the "Great American Desert" in the West.

1843

This first wave of emigrants caused no problems for the Indians. But with the passage of thousands of wagons, **friction** between the two races slowly built, leading to later skirmishes, misunderstandings and massacres.

Today

How much contact do you have with members of another race? If the minority increases to a certain ratio in an area, do you think friction or greater understanding would develop between the races? How can these possible problems be avoided?

Lesson On Avoiding Racial Conflict

Christ can bring **unity** among the races. Paul states, "There is neither Jew nor Greek, slave nor free, male nor female, for you are all **one** in Christ Jesus."(Galatians 3:28) Christ is color blind-we are one in Him.

Related Passages: Matt 18:21-22; Luke 17:3
Col 3:13

June 12

Trying To Change Indians

1843

Most pioneers thought that the Indians should be changed to conform to the white man's idea of civilization. The question was how to accomplish this: "Should you turn the Indian into a Christian and then **civilize** him by teaching him to farm, or would it be better to civilize him first by teaching him the white man's ways and then turn him into an obedient Christian?" **23**

Today

How do you react to the culture of ethnic or racial groups different from you? Do you consider your ways superior, or do you see many things that you can learn from sharing this **diversity**? Do you think you should try to "convert" others different from you to your ways of thinking and "doing culture?" How can we change human behavior?

Lesson On Changing Human Behavior

Paul sees the most effective way to change human behavior is by **renewing** our mind: "Do not conform any longer to the pattern of this world, but be transformed by the renewing of your mind. Then you will be able to test and approve what God's will is-His good, pleasing and perfect will."(Romans 12:2) If our heart, mind and attitudes are changed from the inside, through the power of Christ, then our **actions** will reflect these insights.

Related Passages: Is 43:18-19; Mark 11:25
1 Pet 3:9-10

June 13

Stereotyping Indians

1843

By now the pioneers had encountered Indians from different nations, so their **stereotype** of an Indian as dirty and a beggar was not always accurate. Pierson Reading noted that the Pawnees . . . "bear the character of being a proud and honorable nation. . . best featured Indians I have yet seen. . . they are different from other Indians in one respect, they do not beg." **24**

Today

Do you judge another person's **character** by her/his race, or do you see that person as an individual? Do you find that the more time you spend to get to know people of another race, the more favorably disposed you are toward them? What is the proper way to judge a person's character?

Lesson On Judging Others

Jesus, in His Sermon on the Mount, gave an admonition against judging others: "Do not **judge**, or you too will be judged. For in the same way you judge others, you will be judged. . . "(Matthew 7:1,2) God explains to Samuel how He(God) sees an individual compared to how man sees another person: "The Lord does not look at things man looks at. Man looks at the outward appearance, but the Lord looks at the **heart**."(1 Samuel 16:7). Let's look at others through the eyes of Jesus.

Related Passages: Eph 4:31-32; 5:2,19,30
1John 1:3,7

June 14

Animals Along The Trail

1843

Part of the food the pioneers ate came from animals they hunted along the Trail. The animal which provoked the most interest and curiosity was the **buffalo**, the staple of the Indians. Another type was the **antelope**, very fast and difficult to bring down. These animals provided new challenges to the pioneers, used to raising only domesticated animals.

Today

How important are **animals** to you? Do you see some of them as game to hunt, and others as pets to keep? Are you thankful that the domesticated farm animals provide food and strength, and the birds enrich our lives through their beautiful singing? They are all God's creatures, great and small.

Lesson On Animals

After God created the creatures in the waters, the birds in the air and the animals on the land, He saw them all as **good.** He then gave men power to . . . "rule over the fish of the sea and the birds of the air, over the livestock, over all the earth, and over all the creatures that move along the ground."(Genesis 1: 20-26) Psalm 104:11-30 illustrates how God cares for the animals. We should see them as God's creatures, providing us with both food and enjoyment.

Related Passages: Num 22:28-35; Zech 9:9
Rev 19:11-16

June 15

Flowers Along The Trail

1843

With the wet spring rains, new **wild flowers** emerged on the prairie. These lavender, yellow and white flowers added a colorful variety along the trail. Children would pick them for their parents, adding an aesthetic touch and aromatic smell to the long journey.

Today

Do you take time to "smell the flowers" along the way, or are you caught up in the "tyranny of the urgent?" Do you confuse immediate demands with more important-but less urgent-tasks? "We live in constant tension between the **urgent** and the **important**." **25** How can you balance these two special needs?

Lesson On "Smelling The Flowers"

Jesus, in His Sermon on the Mount, illustrates what is important: "And why do you worry about clothes? See how the **lilies** of the field grow. They do not labor or spin. Yet I tell you that not even Solomon in all his splendor was dressed like one of these. If that is how God clothes the grass of the field, which is here today and tomorrow is thrown into the fire, will He not much more clothe you, O you of little faith?"(Matthew 6:28-30) Here Jesus is saying that (1) real beauty is found in Nature and (2) we should learn from Nature not to worry about our needs. He will provide.

Related Passages: Eccl 3:2; Prov 15:17
Matt 13:31-32

June 16

Herbs Along The Trail

1843

In addition to the flowers, there were **herbs** that could be used for cooking or for medicinal purposes. No doubt the Indians knew more about these native herbs than the pioneers, and may have been willing to share their secrets. Some of the herbs found along the trail included dandelions (leaves could be used as a vegetable and the root for making medicine) and sage (could be used for curing many ailments). **26**

Today

Certain herbs have the potential to be used for **medicinal purposes**. Do you see that they have a valuable purpose for mankind? Or do you see the dandelion as only as a nuisance in your yard? Or you see the sage as only a scrub bush in the desert? How can you see the potential for good in ordinary plants and people?

Lesson On Reaching Our Potential

Jesus came to give us new life that could be used to reach our God-given **potential**. He states His mission as . . . "I have come that they may have life, and have it to the full."(John 10:10) Paul sees the Christian as reaching her/his potential through using inner spiritual gifts. I Corinthians 12 explains the "different kinds of gifts, but the same Spirit."(v 4) Have you found and used your spiritual gift(s) to edify the Church?

Related Passages: Ex 12:5-11; 37:17-24;
Psalm 45:8

June 17

Resting On The Sabbath

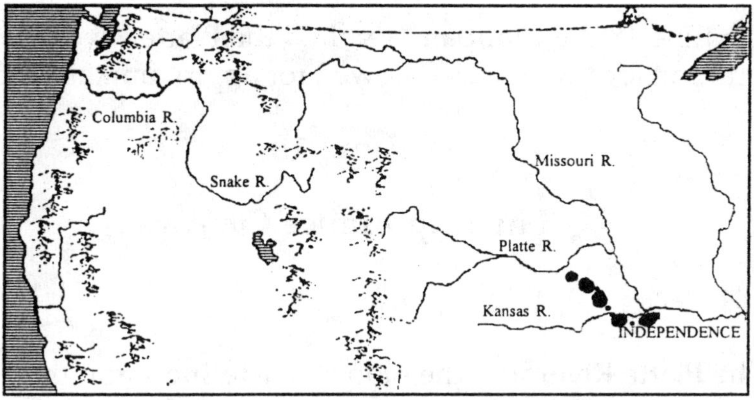

1843

During this week the pioneers followed the Little Blue River from northeast Kansas into southeast Nebraska. They had more than their share of wet weather, good for the animals and flowers, but too much for the Company. It was again time to **rest** themselves and their weary animals.

Today

What is your definition of resting on Sundays? Is it sleeping later and taking a nap, or something else? **Rest** is "not sleeping but ceasing our normal weekly routines. We should pause to compare our priorities. We do this by 'measuring our thoughts and values against the eternal truths that have been revealed through the Scriptures and the mighty acts of God.'" **27** Paul provides guidelines as to what we should be thinking about: . . . "whatever is true, . . . noble, . . . right, . . . pure, . . . lovely, . . . admirable . . . excellent or praiseworthy."(Philippians 4: 8) Great thoughts for a Sunday afternoon stroll.

Related Passages: Prov 24:33; Mt 11:25-30
Heb 4:9-10

Week Five: June 18-24

The Platte River Road

On June 18 the Company reached the Platte River. This natural corridor west was followed for approximately 125 miles.

June 18

The Importance Of Water

1843

The Platte River was the pioneers' **lifeline** through Nebraska. It provided water for the animals and humans, who used it for drinking, cooking and bathing. It was described as " a mile wide and a foot deep," or "too thick to drink and too thin to plow." **28**

Today

How important is **water** to you today? Do you use it at will, or try to conserve its usage? What would happen if the aquifers in the West would run dry? Can we be guaranteed a **source** of water that will never run dry?

Lesson On The Importance Of Water

Jesus used the story of the woman at the well to illustrate the importance of drinking His water: ". . . but whoever drinks the water I give him will never thirst. Indeed, the water I give him will become in him a **spring** of water welling up to eternal life."(John 4:14) Let's allow Jesus to quench our thirst.

Related Passages: Gen 24:10-14; Prov20:5
Jer 2:13

June 19

Monotony On The Plains

1843

The plains along the Platte were so open and flat, and devoid of any variety of landscape, that the journey became **monotonous.** Peter Burnett describes it this way: "In making our monotonous journey up the smooth valley of the Platte, through the warm, genial sunshine of summer, the feeling of drowsiness was so great that it was extremely difficult to keep awake during the day." **29**

Today

It has been said that "**variety** is the spice of life." Is this true for you? Or do you repeat the same thing at your job or home? How can you balance new experiences with your daily routine, and still live an exciting and fulfilling life?

Lesson On Avoiding Monotony

God knows how to make our life exciting as we commit our daily tasks, dreams and goals to Him. Jeremiah 29:11 provides this promise: "For I know the plans I have for you, " declares the Lord, "plans to **prosper** you and not to harm you, plans to give you hope and a future." Jesus challenges us to "abide in Him": "I am the vine; you are the branches. If a man remains in Me and I in him, he will bear much fruit; apart from Me you can do **nothing.**"(John 15:5) The Christian life is the most exciting of all. Have you discovered it?

Related Passages: Ex 12:37-42; Num 14:1-5
Prov 16:9

June 20

Scarcity of Fuel

1843

There were few trees on the "Great American Desert." Therefore the pioneers found a new source of fuel that was plentiful-**buffalo chips**(dung). The children were assigned the dubious responsibility of collecting them each evening. They may even have played Frisbee with them! Nevertheless, they provided a good source of heat for cooking, and were odorless and flameless, like charcoal. So they made do with what they had.

Today

How do you handle unexpected **circumstances** when something or someone in your life changes for the better or the worse? What if you lose your job? Conversely, what if your business does better than projected? What if your spouse leaves you? What if you remarry someone that is just right for you? Do you blame God for the past circumstances, or thank Him for your new situation?

Lesson On Contentment

Paul faced situations of both poverty and prosperity. Here's what he said: "I know what it is to be in need, and I know what it is to have plenty. I have learned the secret of being **content** in any and every situation, whether well fed or hungry, whether living in plenty or in want."(Philippians 4:12) Can you say this in your life too?

Related Passages: Gen 22:1-8; 1 Kings 18:30-39;
Ps 140:10; 148:7-8

June 21

Wind Along The Prairie

1843

And how the **wind** doth blow across the prairies, with no trees to block its path. It was probably a hot wind this time of the year, but at least it kept the bugs away! Because of these winds, cooking had to go underground: "It is necessary to dig a narrow ditch, about eight inches wide, one foot deep, and two or three feet long. This confines the heat and prevents the wind from scattering the fire." **30**

Today

The wind can either be a refreshing breeze on a hot summer day, or cold and biting blast during the winter. Without it, you languish in the heat and humidity. Too much wind and you can have hurricanes and tornadoes. In all cases, you cannot see the wind, only its effects. How important is relying on something you cannot see?

Lesson On The Wind

Jesus uses the mystery of the wind to explain being **born again:** "The wind blows wherever it pleases. You hear its sound, but you cannot tell where it comes from or where it is going. So it is with everyone who is born of the Spirit."(John 3:7-8) We cannot see the Holy Spirit enter a person's life when they ask Christ into their lives, but nonetheless it happens, bringing eternal life and purpose.

Related Passages: Mark 4:35-40; Eph 4:11-16; Js 1:2-8

June 22

Changing Milk Into Butter

1843

The **bumpy ride** across the prairie did have one advantage. For those with milk cows, milk could be churned into butter while traveling. By setting a churn of cream on the back of the wagon, the constant jostling would turn it into butter. This was probably the easiest task of the entire journey.

Today

Have you had certain experiences in your life, which seemed unfortunate initially, but ultimately turned out for your good? Maybe you lost your job, only to find a better one later. Maybe you lost your spouse through divorce or death, only to later find a more compatible partner. How can you turn lemons into lemondade? Or cream into butter?

Lesson On Things Turning Out For Good

Paul provides a promise that things in our life will turn out all right: "And we know that in **all things** God works for the good of those who love Him, who have been called according to His purpose."(Romans 8:28) Peter, in order to make this promise a reality in our life, says we need to eat "**solid food,**" not "milk," since meat "is for the mature, who by constant use have trained themselves to distinguish good from evil."(Hebrews 5:14) Are you drinking "milk" or eating and digesting "solid food" from the Word?

Related Passages: Hab 3:19; 1 Pet 5:7
1 John 5:14-15

June 23

Mosquitoes On The Plains

1843

Traveling near water turned out to be a mixed blessing, since it bred the pesky **mosquitoes.** In the days before spraying and insect repellant, they attacked humans and animals with a vegeance. At least the pioneers had long sleeves, trousers, dresses and hats for partial protection. The animals had no such covering, and could not escape these blood thirsty insects. Another irritant on the Trail.

Today

What things "**bug**" you today? Are they the major problems, like relationships, news events, and financial reversals? Or are they the little things, i.e, barking dogs, cold coffee or not finding your keys? How should we handle the daily nuisances of life? Is it the big "lions and tigers" that get you down, or the small "flies and mosquitoes?"

Lesson On Handling Trials In Life

James offers us this advice in facing **trials:** "Consider it pure joy, my brothers, whenever you face trials of many kinds, because you know that the testing of your faith develops perseverance."(James 1:2-3) Can you be joyful when swatting mosquitoes and flies? Even the seemingly little things in life can be committed to God. After all, not even a sparrow "will fall to the ground apart from the will of your Father."(Matthew 10:29)

Related Passages: Nah 1:7; 2 Cor 4:8-9
Heb 10:35-36

June 24

Socializing On The Sabbath

1843

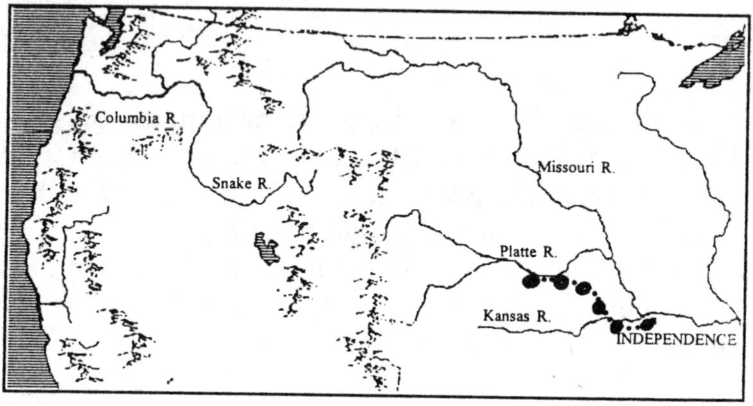

During this week the pioneers endured everything from monotony to mosquitoes. They were beginning to see it was the little things that could get them down. But today they cheered their spirits with "Sunday Socializing," by singing, fiddling and dancing.

Today

Is Sunday different for you than the other six days of the week? Do you take time to visit friends, relatives and family? Do you enjoy singing praises to God at church? Maybe you even "dance in the Spirit." David has a lot to say about singing and dancing to the Lord. We are commanded to "Sing to the Lord . . . "(Psalm 30:4), "Sing joyfully to the Lord . . . " (Psalm 33:1), "Sing praises to God . . " (Psalm 47:6), "Sing the glory of His name . . " (Psalm 66:2) and "Sing to the Lord a new song . . . " (Psalm 96:1). We are even encouraged to ". . . praise His name with dancing and make music to Him with tambourine and harp."(Psalm 149:3). If the pioneers can take time to refresh themselves by singing and dancing, so can we.

Related Passages: 1 Sam 18:10-11; Ps 150
Is 42:10-13

The South Platte Crossing

When the pioneers came to the juncture of the North and South Platte Rivers in today's Nebraska, crossing the latter fork took six days, and proved to be another river challenge.

June 25

Ferrying Across The River

1843

Instead of fording the river, the emigrants tried something new-building **skin boats** made from buffalo hides. By stretching and tacking these skins to their wagon beds, they became ferry boats, capable of being pulled across the wide South Platte.

Today

Do you rush headlong into something, or take more time to figure the situation out, like the pioneers did with their skin boats? Are you spontaneous or deliberate in making decisions?

Lesson On Wisdom

James gives us this advice about **decisions:** "If any of you lacks wisdom he should ask God, who gives generously to all without finding fault, and it will be given him. But when he asks, he must believe and not doubt. . . "(1:5-6) The key is **praying** and **expecting** an answer. Wisdom comes from God(Prov. 1:7).

Related Passages: Prov 24:3-4; Is 43:2
1 Tim 2:1,3,8

June 26

Accidents From Firearms

1843

Because of the rumors of Indian attacks, the pioneer were well fortified with **weapons.** Consequently, the second most common type of accident(after drownings) was carelessness in using firearms. "Several overlanders acknowledged that they were much more frightened of carelessly handled guns in their own trains than they were of any hostile Indians." **31**

Today

Have you experienced serious **accidents**, inflicted during a storm, while driving an automobile or falling on the ice? How do you handle these unplanned events? Do you become bitter and blame God, or look for "the good" in them?

Lesson On Responding To Accidents

If anyone had the right to complain, it was the Biblical character Job. In rapid succession, he lost all his family and possessions to storms and attackers.(Job 1) What was his response to these concurrent tragedies? "Naked I came from my mother's womb, and naked I will depart. The Lord gave and the Lord has taken away; may the name of the Lord be **praised.**(1:21) "Shall we accept good from God, and not trouble?"(2:10) Can we respond like Job, realizing that the Christian life does not immunize us from suffering?

Related Passages: Psalm 103:3; Luke 6:19
3 John 2

June 27

Clouds

1843

The time following the Platte River was one of relative monotony. The scenery, with its endless, flat prairie was repetitious. The elevation gain across Nebraska averaged ten feet per mile-a fairly easy ascent. During these lazy days of summer, the emigrants no doubt looked up at the bright, white fluffy **cloud** formations, envisioning shapes of animals, people and rocks. This was a welcome diversion to looking down at the dusty trail all day. It expanded their horizons.

Today

During your busy schedule, do you take time to look up at the clouds, dreaming of what you can become? Looking at white, billowy clouds seems to create an atmosphere for relaxation and reflection. Some day we will see something **spectacular** in the clouds. Are you ready for it?

Lesson On Looking Up

The Bible states that Jesus is coming again "in a cloud with great power and glory,"(Luke 21:27) His Second Coming will not be missed by anyone: "Look, He is coming with the clouds, and every eye will see Him, even those who pierced Him; and all the peoples of the earth will mourn because of Him. "(1:7) Whereas Jesus came the first time as a baby, He will come again as a **king.** Are you ready?

Related Passages: Ps 36:5-6; Dan 7:13-14
Heb 12:1; Rev 1:7-8

June 28

Readers Went To Oregon

1843

Most of the families traveling to Oregon must have been able to **read**. According to a myth, a sign consisting of two arrows stood at the point where the Oregon and California Trails divided. "One arrow pointed due west with the words 'To Oregon' painted on it, and the other pointed south-west with a simple drawing of a pile of quartz." **32** Those that could read presumably went to Oregon, while the others went to the California gold fields.

Today

How important is reading to you? What types of written materials do you read-newspapers, magazines or books? What types of books do you mainly prefer, nonfiction or fiction? How many authors do you personally know? The Bible is a **nonfiction** book where you must first know the author to understand the content. How can you know the author, and better understand what you read?

Lesson On Studying The Bible

In order to make reading the Bible more meaningful, you must first know the **author**(God) and sincerely asking Jesus to direct your life. The Holy Spirit will then give you a desire to read and study His Word. Maybe you will emulate the Bereans who "examined the Scriptures every day to see if what Paul said was true."(Acts 17:11) Set this as your goal.

Related Passages: Acts 7:17-22; 1 Cor 2:6-16
Phil 2:5-11

June 29

Gradual Ascent To South Pass

1843

The journey from Independence, Missouri(800 feet elevation) to South Pass(7,500 feet elevation) was one of gradually gaining elevation. Each successive state experienced a **steadily increasing gain**-Kansas, 200 feet; Nebraska, 3,200 feet; and Wyoming, 3,500 feet gain. Overall the wagons gained approximately 7,000 feet in elevation in 900 miles-an average of eight feet per mile. No wonder the animals and people tired!

Today

What is the highest elevation you have ascended, either hiking, biking, or driving an automobile? In a car you would harldly know you were climbing; hiking or biking would be a different story! Is your **spiritual walk** one of gradually getting closer to God, or do you have peaks and valleys in your Christian journey?

Lesson On Christian Growth

The Christian life begins when you accept Christ into your life. You then grow closer to Him as you read His Word, pray to Him, fellowship with other Christians and tell others about Him. As you do these things, asking for His power, you can begin to identify with Paul as he challenged the Colossians to "live a life worthy of the Lord . . . pleasing Him in every way: bearing fruit in every good work, growing in the knowledge of God."(1:10) There's no better goal than this. Are you ascending in your elevated walk with Him?

Related Passages: Is 58:10-11; Rom 8:16-17
I Pet 1:3-4

June 30

Necessities Versus Luxuries

1843

As the oxen plodded higher and higher, the wagon load became heavier and heavier. Even though the original 2,500 pounds may have included such "necessities" as a dresser or cast iron stove, these items by now were considered luxuries. In order to preserve the stamina of the faithful oxen, these items were jettisoned by the trail, leaving them for followers or the Indians. The "greatest litterbugs in American history," they were called. **33**

Today

When making purchases today, how do you determine what are necessities and what are luxuries? Do you need more than one automobile? How big of a house do you need? Do you buy based on your **needs**, or because you **want** to "keep up with the neighbors?" In our materialistic culture, with its saturation advertising, wants are portrayed as needs. How can we focus on important needs instead of luxurious wants?

Lesson On Supplying Our Needs

Exodus(Chapter 16) provides an excellent example of how the Israelites' needs were met in the desert. For six days each week the Lord provided quail during the evening, and manna in the morning. The people were to gather as much as they **needed** each day. If they kept part of their daily portion until the next day, it spoiled so they could not eat it. On the sixth day they were to gather twice as much for the Sabbath, and this portion did not spoil. This was God's method of providing for their needs for **forty years-one day at a time**! God promises to also supply our needs-sometimes it may be just in the nick of time!

Related Passages: Rom 8:16-17; Gal 3:29
Heb 11:16

July 1

Reflecting On Our Priorities

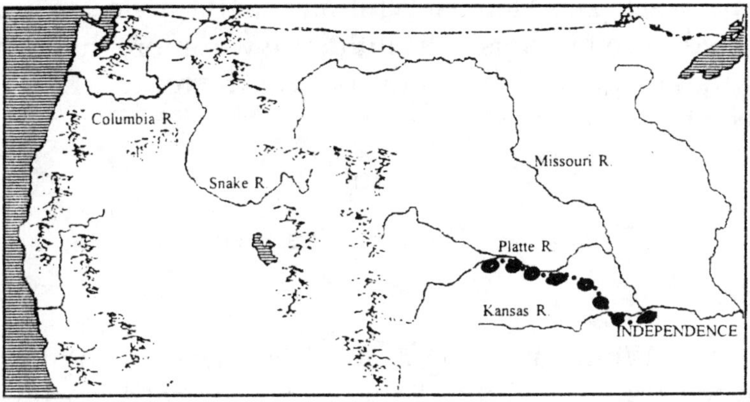

1843

Rivers once again played a big part in the journey. The pioneers spent six days crossing the South Platte River. It was now time to reflect on how far they had come, and how far they had to go. They were less than one-third of the way to Oregon.

Today

MacDonald recommends pausing on Sunday "to compare our priorities." We can do this by "measuring our **thoughts** and values against the eternal truths that have been revealed through the Scriptures and the mighty acts of God." **34** Paul gives us the formula for how we should **think**: ". . . whatever is right, whatever is pure, whatever is lovely, whatever is admirable-if anything is excellent or praiseworthy-think about such things."(Phil 4:8) Is this our thought life? Maybe we should use Sunday to reflect about what occupies our thinking-a worthy introspection!

Related Passages: Deut 1:30; Is 55:10-11
1 Pet 1:24-25

The Missionary Doctor

This week Dr. Marcus Whitman, a Presbyterian minister, joined the emigrants. His influence was more than spiritual, in that he guided the pioneers over the route where he had been twice before.

July 2

Healing The Sick

1843

Marcus Whitman, being a physician, was much in demand on the Trail. Even though modern medical science was not developed in the 1840s, Whitman's skills and **frontier** medicines were still appreciated.

Today

Doctors play an important role in healing the sick. Even though they seem to occupy a high status in society, they are not important to you until you need their expertise. How important are doctors to you in curing your ills? Do you rely on the **natural healing** of the body? How important is **prayer**?

Lesson On Needing A Physician

Jesus related the need for a doctor to man's sinful nature. He was criticized by the Pharisees for associating with the tax collectors and "sinners." When questioned about this practice, Jesus responded, "It is not the healthy who need a doctor, but the sick. . . For I have not come to call the righteous, but **sinners.**(Matt 9:12-3) Do we mainly associate with the people who go to church with us, and seem righteous, or do we go out "into the highways and byways," bringing people to Christ?

Related Passages: Ex 15:26; Matt 9:35
I Pet 2:24; James 5:14-15

July 3

Combining The Sacred And The Secular

1843

Marcus Whitman, with his new bride Narcissa, was traveling West with Reverend Henry Spalding, and his wife Eliza. Their goal was to establish a **mission** to Christianize the Native Americans. Even though their call was a sacred one, they had to attend to the many practical affairs of organizing and running a mission. Thus synthesizing the spiritual with the sacred was important to their new venture.

Today

How do you combine the spiritual and secular aspects of your life? Do you attend church on Sunday to fulfill your sacred responsibilities, and forget about God during the week? Or do you stay in contact with Him throughout the week by having a regular "quiet time," and being aware of **His presence** moment-by-moment?

Lesson On Not Segmenting Our Lives

Paul encourages us to take a **holistic approach** to life by stating, "So whether you eat or drink or whatever you do, do it all to the glory of God."(1 Cor 10:31) Even though Paul realizes we must live in the world, our weapons are spiritual: "For though we live in the world, we do not wage war as the world does. The weapons we fight with are not the weapons of the world. On the contrary, they have divine power to demolish strongholds."(2 Cor 3:4) As Christians, we really do have the **best** of both worlds!

Related Passages: Jer 33:3; Ps 91:15
John 14:13;Eph 6

July 4

Celebrating "The Glorious Fourth"

1843

Instead of relaxing at Independence Rock on the **Fourth of July,** as did later wagon trains, the Great Migration was moving across the South Platte. James Nesmith recorded, " The glorious Fourth had once more rolled around. Myself, with most of our company, celebrated it by swimming and fording the South fork of the Big Platte, with cattle, wagons, baggage and so forth." **35** Continuing the journey took precedence over the biggest holiday of the year.

Today

How do you celebrate the Fourth? Do you enjoy a picnic with family and friends, culminating in the "biggest fire-works display in the area?" Do you pause to reflect upon the meaning of this historic event, and the risks the **Founding Fathers** made to secure our freedoms, including the right to worship God as we desire? How do we balance **freedom** with **responsibility** in society?

Lesson On Freedom And Responsibility

One of Paul's major themes is to contrast the old life of bondage to sin with the new life of freedom in Christ. In Romans he states, "Therefore, there is now no condemnation for those who are in Christ Jesus, because through Christ Jesus the law of the Spirit of life set me **free** from the law of sin and death."(8:12) In Galatians 5 Paul balances freedom in Christ with responsibility when he cautions Christians to "not use your freedom to indulge the sinful nature."(v 13) In a seeming paradox, we gain more freedom as we **yield** more of our lives to the control of Christ.

Related Passages: Col 4:1; 1 Thess 4:10-12
Heb 13:15-16

July 5

"White Man's Book Of Heaven"

1843

In 1831 four Indians journeyed to St. Louis with a fur-trading party returning from their annual rendezvous. They were looking for the "white man's book of heaven." This "**Macedonian cry**" reached Marcus Whitman, who responded five years later by traveling West to establish a mission to the Cayuse Indians near present Walla Walla, Washington.

Today

In the United States, we have an abundance of Bibles, with various translations. All you have to do is visit your local Christian book store. You can even stay in a motel and read a Gideon Bible free! How many Bibles do you own? How **important** is this book to you? Would you travel many miles, as did these Indians, to learn about this unique book?

Lesson On The Importance Of The Bible

When presenting the Gospel to others, it is important to read or speak using Bible verses. We have the following promise in Isaiah that our efforts will be fruitful: "As the rain and snow come down from heaven, and do not return to it without watering the earth and making it bud and flourish, so that it yields seed for the sower and bread for the eater, so is my **word** that goes out from my mouth: It will not return to me empty, but will accomplish what I desire."(55:10,11) We can't go wrong by **quoting Scripture**.

Related Passages: John 5:39; Heb 4:12
1 Pet 1:24-25

July 6

The "Macedonian Cry"

1843

The Whitmans and Spaldings responded to preach the Gospel to the "uttermost part of the world"(which the West seemed to be in the 1840s). They could have stayed back in the civilized East, content to keep their "secure" jobs. But in the pioneer spirit, they risked a **new venture,** convinced they were "called" for this new work.

Today

Have you ever thought of giving up the security of a good job, many of your possessions, and the familiarity of family and friends to "launch out into the deep" of a new job in a different area? Are you **walking close** with God so that you have heard His "call?" How have you responded to His "voice?"

Lesson On Responding To God's "Call"

Both the Old and New Testaments provide examples of how God's messengers responded to God's "call" to preach the Gospel. When Isaiah "heard the voice of the Lord saying, 'Whom shall I send? And who will go for us?' (he) said, 'Here am I. Send me!"(Is 6:8) When the Apostle Paul "had a vision of a man of Macedonia standing and begging him, 'Come over to Macedonia and help us,' . . . (he) got ready at once to leave for Macedonia, concluding that God had called us to **preach** the Gospel to them."(Acts 16:9-10) We need to be **sensitive** to God's "call" on our lives, and to respond quickly.

Related Passages: Neh 9:20; Josh 1:8
Prov 6:22-23; Ps 16:3

July 7

Sterling Character

1843

Marcus Whitman, a physician, was described by James Nesmith as possessing "a great and good heart, full of charity and courage, and utterly destitute of cant, hypocrisy, shams and effeminancy, and always terribly in **earnest.**" Jesse Applegate credits Dr. Whitman for the successful conclusion of their journey. **36** Marcus Whitman was a man of the highest character, living what he was preaching.

Today

How many ministers do you know who have unquestioned character? Are they the same person in secret as they are behind the public pulpit? Character demands consistency and integrity. Do you possess it? If not, how can you obtain **genuine character**?

Lesson On Obtaining Character

The Apostle Paul sees character on a continuum from hope to suffering: "And we rejoice in the hope of the glory of God. Not only so, but we also rejoice in our sufferings, because we know that suffering produces perseverance, perseverance, **character**; and character, hope."(Romans 5:3-4) Therefore character is obtained through a process of our rejoicing in the good as well as the bad times. Through the Holy Spirit we can cultivate character.

Related Passages: Ecc 7:8-9; Rom 8:38-39
Gal 5:22-23

July 8

Reflecting On The End Of Your Life

1843

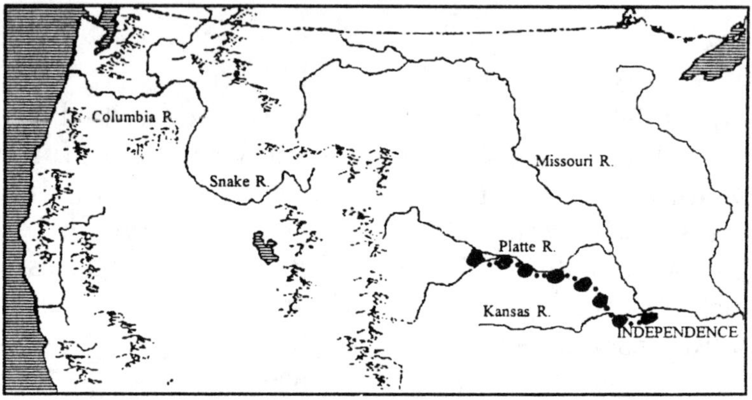

Marcus Whitman died a martyr's death in 1847 at his mission near present Walla Walla, Washington. The Cayuse Indians, to whom Whitman was ministering, died from **measles**, since they had no immunity to this white man's disease. Meanwhile the whites recovered. The Cayuse interpreted this to mean Dr. Whitman was deliberately killing them. They attacked the mission, murdering Marcus and Narcissa Whitman and 11 others. **37** A tragic misunderstanding!

Today

Ponder this sobering question on the Sabbath: Would you be willing to minister in an area that could end in a **martyr's death**? All of Christ's 11 faithful disciples, except one(John) died a violent death because of their allegiance to their Savior. Hebrews 11:35-7 graphically records the types of deaths the saints were subjected to because of their faith in God. Would you give your life for your faith, knowing that "God had planned something better for us. . . ?"(Hebrews 11: 40)

Related Passages: Is 61:1-3; 2 Cor 1:3-4
1 Thess 4:13-14; Rev 21;4

Sights Along The North Platte

After traveling 500 miles, the emigrants finally saw scenery they had not encountered on their farms. They were awestruck by the landmarks they saw. These aesthetic aspects of the journey rejuvenated them for the rigors they were soon to face.

July 9

A Voluntary Migration: Making A Choice

1843

The pioneers trip to Oregon was unlike any other journey in our nation's history. It was "the longest **voluntary** mass migration in the history of the United States." **38** No government edict forced these families to head West. These emigrants exercised their **freedom of choice** , and were willing to accept the consequences of settling in the Willamette Valley, or perishing along the way.

Today

We live in a country that affords us the same freedom of choice experienced by the pioneers. We can start a new business, as long as we realize the consequences-either success or failure. What major choices have you made in your life?

Lesson On Making Choices

All of life is making choices. The most important choice we will ever make is where we will spend eternity-either with Christ in heaven, or with Satan in hell. "God has given us eternal life, and this life is in His Son. He who has the Son has life; he who does not have the Son of God does not have life."(I John 5:11-12) Where have you chosen to spend eternity?

Related Passages: Ps 37:18; 1 Cor 15:54-55
1 Jn 5:20

July 10

Strong-Willed Independent Pioneers

1843

Even though the pioneers started out as one large wagon train, they eventually split into a collection of smaller groups of wagons. After seven weeks on the Trail, they formed "cliques" with those they liked, or trusted. "That was a hard-nosed attitude to be sure, but these were tough, independent people. After all, the timid and inflexible had never left home." **39**

Today

Do you admire the dominant and decisive or the docile and "submissive" personalities? Today's movie and television heroes are portrayed as figuring things out for themselves, and overcoming insurmountable obstacles to reach the "top." They are definitely strong-willed and independent characters.

Lesson On Admirable Characteristics

Jesus' Sermon on the Mount call certain characteristics **blessed.** Among them are persons who are poor in spirit, who mourn, who are meek, who hunger and thirst for righteousness, are merciful, are pure in heart, are peacemakers and are persecuted because of their righteousness.(Matt 5:3-10) These characteristics are a far cry from those usually admired by society. What characteristics typify you-those of society or those emulated by Jesus?

Related Passages: 2 Chron 5:13-14; Prov 24:3-4;
1 Thess 4:10-12

July 11

Courthouse Rock

1843

The pioneers saw **Courthouse and Jail Rocks** simultaneously, since they were adjacent to each other. Rufus Sage describes Courthouse Rock as follows: "It rises in an abrupt quadrilangular form, to a height of three or four hundred feet, and covers an area of two hundred yards in length by one hundred and fifty broad. Occupying a perfectly level site in an open prairie, it stands as the proud place of Solitude, amid here boundless domains." **40**

Today

Of the three branches of our government, the **judicial branch** seems to draw the most interest. Witness the plethora of books, movies and television programs pertaining to cops and courtroom dramas. You surely remember several trials of the century. What does the Bible have to say about obeying laws and leaders?

Lesson On Obeying Leaders And Laws

Paul commands the Christians in Rome "to **submit** to the authorities, not only because of possible punishment but also because of conscience."(13:5) Peter declares: "Submit yourselves for the Lord's sake to every authority instituted among men. . . "(I Peter 2:13) Contrary to popular sentiment, laws are meant to be obeyed, not broken. Do you obey?

Related Passages: Ex 17:1-7; Is 32:1-4
Gal 5:7-15

July 12

Jail Rock

1843

When he saw **Courthouse Rock** and **Jail Rock**, Overton Johnson wrote: "There are here several ranges of detached Sand Hills . . . the sides of which are almost perpendicular, destitute of vegetation, and so washed by the ruins of thousands of years, as to present . . . the appearances of Cities, Temples, Castles, Towers, Palaces, and every variety of great and magnificent structures." **41**

Today

Prisons are also part of our judicial system, used to mete out justice to convicted criminals. Is justice even- handed and effective as a deterrent to future crimes, or is it a breeding ground for learning about more serious crimes? What type of **justice** is pictured in the Bible?

Lesson On Justice

God is a God of justice(Isaiah 30:18) and therefore must punish sin. The Book of Revelation describes the justice of God at work against those who have rejected His son, who was sent to **atone** for our sins. At the Great White Throne Judgment, probably the saddest verse of the Bible is recorded: "If anyone's name was not found written in the **Book of Life**, he was thrown into the lake of fire."(Revelation 22:14). May these words not be uttered against you or your loved ones.

Related Passages: Deut 29:20-22; Rom 2:1-16;
2 Pet 3:10-18

July 13

Chimney Rock

1843

Fifteen miles further west was **Chimney Rock**, the landmark occupying more diary space than any other natural formation. According to Nesmith, "(it) resembles a funnel reversed" and is, "one of the greatest curiosities I have ever seen in the West." Newby said it "Looks like a chimney." **42**

Today

Chimney's today are an integral part of your home's heating system, especially if you are using wood. Chimney's need to be swept periodically to eliminate creosote that could cause a chimney fire. What types of **residues** need to be eliminated in your life, so that you can more effectively be a witness for Christ?

Lesson On Laying Aside Distractions

What hinderances and sins keep you from being fully committed to Christ? worrying about finances? preoccupation with your job? too much television? your thought life? accumulating too many "toys?" The writer of Hebrews encourages Christians to . . . "throw off everything that hinders and the sin that so easily entangles, and let us run with perseverance the race marked out for us."(12:1) First eliminate your **"creosote;"** Then you can run the "race of life" with His persevering power. Be clean at the start!

Related Passages: Is 8:12-22; Matt 7:24-28
Luke 8:4-8

July 14

Scotts Bluff

1843

Twenty miles west of Chimney Rock loomed **Scotts Bluff,** rising 700 feet from the surrounding plateau. This formation was named for Hiram Scott, who in 1828 became ill, and was left for dead by his companions. The next summer it was discovered that Scott did not die where he was left, but had crawled several miles before dying. He was tragically **abandoned** by his "friends!"

Today

Have you ever seen an accident on the highway, and wondered whether or not to stop and render assistance? Would it make a difference if no one else had stopped? Would you still stop if others were there? Many states have laws requiring you to render assistance in these situtations. When should you be a "**Good Samaritan**?"

Lesson On Being A "Good Samaritan"

The parable of the Good Samaritan(Luke 10:30-37) illustrates who is our neighbor-**anyone** whom we know is in need of assistance. This story indicates we show His love by helping the unfortunate, regardless of race or religion. The parable concludes that we can't wait for someone else to "help out." Even the priest and the Levite didn't stop. Therefore, it's up to us to be "Good Samaritans." Who are you in the story?

Related Passages: Ps 27:14; 138:7; Js 3:16-18
1 Jn 4:18

July 15

Landmarks In Our Lives

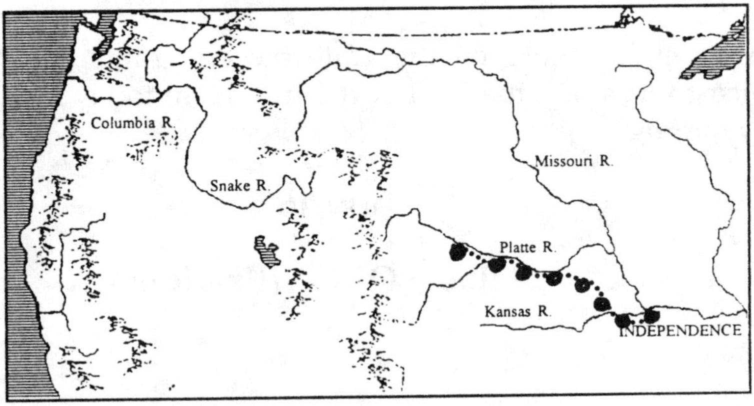

1843

The emigrants had traveled 600 miles by the time they had passed the landmarks in Western Nebraska-roughly one-third of their way to Oregon. This Sabbath would be a good time for them to assess their progress on the journey. Did they need to make any **changes** for the more rugged terrain ahead?

Today

Have you taken time to assess your life. One method would be to reflect on each decade of your life(30s, 40s, etc.) to answer questions in the following four areas:

Physical-How physically fit am I?

Social- Am I meeting my family's needs? Am I aquiring meaningful relationships?

Intellectual-Have I met the requirments for the educational degree(s) I want to achieve? Am I a lifelong learner, using my God-given gifts and abilities?

Spiritual-Have I made a personal commitment to my God? Am I growing in my relationship with Christ? Where is the Lord leading me in ministering to others? **43**

Related Passages: Eph 4:31-32; 6:10-20
Jude 24,25

Week Nine: July 16-July 22

Fort Laramie

After eight weeks on the Trail, the emigrants enjoyed the nicest fort along the Trail-**Fort Laramie**, in today's southeast Wyoming.

July 16

A Taste Of Civilization

1843

Fort Laramie, with its gas lights and high walls, was a favorite with the women. They could dust off their dresses, get **"gussied up"** and "promenade" along the parade grounds. They momentarily thought they were back East, enjoying their former civilized customs.

Today

Are there times when you like to dress up and "do the town?" Sometimes it just feels good to clean up and put on some **new** clothes. What does Jesus require of us before we can approach Him?

Lesson On "Cleaning Up To Meet Jesus"

Jesus **accepts** us the way we are. He doesn't expect us to dress up before we can come into His presence. As the popular hymn says, "Just as I am, without one plea, but that Thy blood is shed for me. . . " As Paul explains in Romans, "But God demonstrates His own love for us in this: While we were still sinners, Christ died for us."(5:8) **Come as you are!**

Related Passages: Ps 51:1-2; Is 61:10; Joel 2:12-13
Matt 9:15-17; 2 Cor 7:1; 1 John 1:7,9

July 17

The Protection Of Fort Laramie

1843

John C. Fremont describes Fort Laramie thus: ". . . its lofty walls, whitewashed and picketed, with the large bastions at the angles, gave it quite an imposing appearance . . . the fort, which is a quadrangular structure, built of clay . . . walls are about fifteen feet high, surmounted with a wooden palisade, and form a portion of ranges of houses, which entirely surround a yard of about one hundred and thirty feet square."
44

Today

Today we don't live in **forts**, but we still build fences for privacy. For protection we install security systems, complete with automatic lights and alarms linked to the police station. Crime is a real concern in most urban areas. From where does our real security come?

Lesson On Protection

Several references in the Old Testament speak of **forts** as protection. The prophet Samuel compares Jehovah to His fortress.(II Samuel 22:2) David sees "The Lord as my fort where I can enter and be safe . . . my tower of strength and safety."(Psalms 18:2 and 144:2) Our security is **in Christ** and not in man-made systems. Is this where your security lies?

Related Passages: Deut 33:26-29; Ps 91
Jer 16:19

July 18

Restoration At Fort Laramie

1843

For most pioneers reaching the destination in Oregon was more important than enjoying the journey. However, the safety and amenities of Fort Laramie allowed them to "smell the wildflowers along the way." During this brief **respite** the men could use the blacksmith and carpentry shops to repair their wheels, while the women caught up on the laundry, quilting and other domestic chores. **45**

Today

In the midst of your hectic schedule, when do you take time to "enjoy the journey?" Are you caught up in the "tyranny of the urgent," giving attention to activities that are urgent but not important. Stephen Covey recommends devoting time to activities(building relationships, planning and recreation) that are **important** but not urgent. **46** In what important or urgent activities do you engage daily?

Lesson On An Important Activity

Probably the best way to prepare for each day is to have a **meditation time** with your Lord- reading His Word, listening to His voice and praying. Read David's account of his meditation: "In the morning, O Lord, you hear my voice; in the morning I lay my requests before you, and wait in expectation."(Psalm 5:3) When do you have your "quiet time?"

Related Passages: Josh 1:8; Col 2:2; 3:16
Heb 10:24-25; 1 John 1:3,7

July 19

High Prices At Fort Laramie

1843

The emigrants could stock up on supplies, but paid comparatively **high prices**. Peter Burnett found coffee and brown sugar at $1.50 a pint; flour, 25 cents a pound; powder, $1.50 per pound; lead, 75 cents per pound; percussion caps, $1.50 per box; and calico, $1.00 a yard. Scarcity and lack of competition explained these exorbitant prices. **47**

Today

When are you willing to pay excessive prices for goods? What about buying fruit out of season? Remember the gas lines and high prices during the Arab Oil Embargo of the 1970s? Do you pay "scalper's" rates for big game football, basketball or baseball tickets? What is the **highest price** you are willing to pay for something valuable?

Lesson On Paying The Highest Price

Jesus paid the highest price possible for us. He gave **His life** so that we wouldn't have to spend eternity in hell. The Gospel message is summed up in the well-known verse, "For God so loved the world that He gave His one and only Son, that whoever believes in Him shall not perish but have eternal life."(John 3: 16) Now that's **real love**! Are you thankful He paid the ultimate price?

Related Passages: Mark 16:15-16; John 15:13
Acts 16:32

July 20

"Go-backs"

1843

Around this point in the journey some decided to turn east and head back to their homes. They **lost faith** and **courage,** "Their hearts weakened at the prospect of the toil, privations and dangers of the trip and the great uncertainty of its termination. . . I am of the opinion that those who turned back manifested more discretion, but less valor than those of us who braved the dangers and uncertainties of the trip." **48**

Today

Have there been times when you started toward a professional or personal goal, only to reverse yourself and go the opposite way? Was this **discretion** the better part of valor, or did you lack the faith and perseverance to continue? How do you know when to continue, or when to change your course of action?

Lesson On Changing Your Course

Jesus has these harsh words for Christians who are not seeking to become His disciples: "No one who puts his hand to the plow and looks **back** is fit for service in the Kingdom of God."(Luke 9:62) However, God promises to cure us of our backsliding if we will return to Him.(Jeremiah 3:22) Do you want to grow with Christ in a consistent walk with Him?

Related Passages: Job 36:11; Matt 6:33
Mark 10:29-30; 3 John 2

July 21

The Courage To Continue

1843

Of the 875 men, women and children who started for Oregon, only 5 to 8 were "go-backs." **49** The vast majority had a vision of the "promised land," and the **courage** to complete the journey. They had been on the trail long enough now to face the dangers with self-confidence. Fort Laramine bolstered their spirits to continue.

Today

When in your life have you needed the courage to face a particular situation? Was it an emergency, such as an accident, requiring quick-thinking, or a long-term commitment such as a serious illness? From where does courage come? How **deep** must you reach?

Lesson On Courage

The Book of Acts records many instances of courage. When Paul was shipwrecked by a storm, he exhorted and prophesied to the other men on the ship to ". . . keep up your courage, men, for I have **faith** in God that it will happen just as He (angel of God) told me."(27:25) Paul also links faith in God with courage and other attributes in I Corinthians: "Be on your guard; stand firm in the faith; be men of courage; be strong."(16:13) God can give you the courage to face any situation.

Related Passages: Gen 28:15; Matt 6:20-21
I Cor 10:13

July 22

Reflecting At Red Buttes

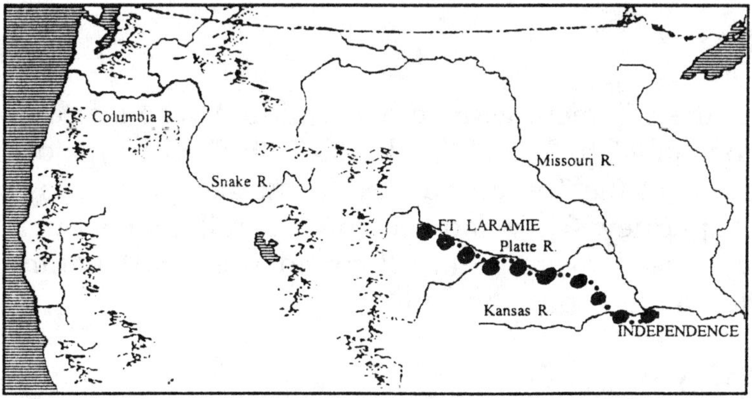

1843

The emigrants passed through a beautiful area known as Red Buttes, described by Overton Johnson as, "occupying a space of many miles in extent, and a large portion of the earth and stone, or which they are composed, is as red as **blood**." On this Sunday they had reached the spot where they were to ford the north fork of the Platte River, 736 miles from Missouri, where they started. **50**

Today

Some agnostics criticize Christianity because it seems to focus on the blood of Jesus, and His horrible death on the cross. But it is only through His **blood atonement** than we are spared a horrible eternal death in hell. Romans provides an explanation: "God presented Him as a sacrifice of atonement, through faith in His blood."(3:25) "Since we have now been justified by His blood, how much more shall we be saved from God's wrath through Him!"(5:9) If the shedding of Jesus' blood could have been avoided, God would have thought of another way.

Related Passages: Rom 5:6-11; Eph 1:7-12
Col 1:19-23

Independence Rock

The lack of good water, dust and the summer **heat** challenged the emigrants during this week. However, they were able to enjoy a significant landmark-Independence Rock.

July 23

Alkali

1843

The emigrants encountered **salty pools** of water-undrinkable for both man and beast. Overton Johnson wrote, we suffered considerably for the want of water-the little we found(was) strongly impregnated with a kind of salt, prevalent almost everywhere. . . " **51**

Today

Have you ever tasted water from the ocean? How about from the Great Salt Lake, which is nine times saltier than the oceans? Bitter, huh? But **salt** has it's good features as well.

Lesson On Being "Salt"

Jesus says His disciples are the "salt of the earth." He warns us not to "lose (our) saltiness, . . . otherwise we are "no longer good for anything."(Matthew 5:13) Are you the world's "salt," or have you lost your "spice?"

Related Passages: Num 18:19-20; Is 35:7
Mark 9:50; Col 4:2-6

July 24

Dust

1843

Whereas the emigrants faced the problem of **mud** during the spring, **dust** was the culprit in the dryness of summer. There was no escaping it-it would accumulate on their families, animals and wagons. The clouds of dust made visibility a problem. That's why the wagons spread out, to avoid eating each others dust. Their eyes became red and their clothes turned gray.

Today

If you live in the West you have probably experienced dust storms. Sometimes even the roads are closed, and you have to turn on your headlights for visibility. The dust even seeps into your homes, keeping the cleaning lady busy. It is not a valued commodity, but a nuisance to be tolerated. What does **dust** symbolize in the Bible?

Lesson On The Importance Of Dust

Dust in the Bible signifies the temporal aspect of human existence. Since "God formed . . . man from the dust of the ground,"(Genesis 2:7), we will return to the ground, since from it (we) were taken; for dust we are and to dust you will return."(Genesis 3:19) Even though our body will die and decay in the ground, our soul will **live** on. Will your soul go to heaven or hell?

Related Passages: Ps 22:15; Matt 10:11-15
Rev 18:19-20

July 25

Heat

1843

The **heat** of summer added to the misery index through central Wyoming. Sunburn and dehydration were the by-products of the constantly high temperatures. Here's where sunscreen and water bottles would come in handy! The emigrants had no place to hide from the elements during the day. They no doubt welcomed any shade and the setting sun.

Today

What are the hottest **temperatures** you have experienced? Have you been in a sustained heat wave of over 100 degrees? How much of that time were you outside compared to an air-conditioned environment? What if you couldn't escape the heat?

Lesson On Heat and Fire

In Jesus' story of the rich man and Lazarus, the realities of hell are graphically illustrated.(Luke 16: 19-31) While the rich man was in hell, he called to Father Abraham: "Have pity on me and send Lazarus(who is in heaven) to dip the tip of his finger in water and cool my tongue, because I am in agony in this fire."(v. 24) The worst part of this story is that hell is permanent-a great **chasm** prevents anyone from crossing over to heaven. On which side of the chasm are you? your relatives? your friends? Only in **this lifetime** is there time to accept Christ.

Related Passages: Ps 139:7-12; Matt 5:27-30
2 Pet 2:4-11

July 26

Willow Springs

1843

After two days of fighting dust, dehydration and heat the emigrants came to Willow Springs, described by Johnson as, "a beautiful **spring**, of very clear cold water, rising in a green valley, through which its water flows about one mile, and sinks in the sand." **52** This was an actual spring, not a mirage.

Today

Have you been traveling on a hot summer day, only to find an actual spring by the side of the road? Have you taken a drink of these refreshing waters? We obtain our drinking water from a spring close to where we live. It is cold, pure and quenches our thirst temporarily. What if we could **drink** water that would satisfy our longings **permanently**?

Lesson On "Living Water"

The Book of Jeremiah refers to God as "the spring of living water."(3:12) When Jesus encountered the Samaritan woman at the well(John 4: 4-26), He contrasted well water with His water: "Everyone who drinks this(well) water will be thirsty again, but whoever drinks the water I give him will **never thirst**. Indeed the water I give him will become in him a **spring** of water welling up into eternal life."(vv. 13-14) Have you received Jesus' pure eternal water?

Related Passages: Ps 1:1-3; Is 41:17
Mark 16:15-20

July 27

Sweetwater River

1843

On this day the pioneers found more water, a tributary of the North Platte named the Sweetwater River-so named because a fur-trapper's mule fell into these waters, losing a pack of sugar. **53** This was a pure and cold **stream** that provided a welcome source of water after the alkali pools. How "**sweet** it was!"

Today

What things or happenings are "**sweet**" to you? Is it the unexpected visit of a long-lost friend? How about enjoying a refreshing "smoothie" on a hot summer day? How about when your boss says you can leave early Friday afternoon? It is the little pleasant surprises in life that add zest and variety to living. What is seen as "sweet" in the Bible?

Lesson On Sweetness

David sees God's words as sweet "to my taste, sweeter than honey to my mouth."(Psalm 119:103) Solomon, in the Book of Proverbs, relates sweetness to honey in two instances. He sees "A longing fulfilled (as) sweet to the soul . . ."(13:19), and "Pleasant words (as being) a honeycomb, sweet to the soul and healing to the bones."(16:24) Do your words match the "sweetness" of God's message?

Related Passages: Lev 1:3-9; Is 5:20
Eph 5:1-2

July 28

The "Registry of the Desert"

1843

Some of the emigrants painted their **names** on Independence Rock, which looked like a giant turtle 1,900 feet long, 700 feet wide and 128 feet high. Rufus Sage, disgusted with seeing many other names on the Rock, resolved, "If there be no other mode of immortalizing myself, I will be content to descend to the grave unhonored and unsung." **54**

Today

Today individuals still carve or paint their names on rocks or trees as individuals or as couples, announcing a budding romance. These persons want to leave their "**mark** in the world" after they are gone. What kind of name recognition do you want to leave behind?

Lesson On Leaving A Good Name(Reputation)

Solomon emphasizes the importance of a good name or reputation by comparing it to gold: "A good name is more desirable than great riches; to be esteemed better than silver or gold."(Proverbs 22:1) In Ecclesiastes he compares a good name to perfume: "A good name is better than fine perfume."(7:1) Our **reputation** will always precede us to a new location, or be left behind when we move. Thus, no matter where you may be, you will be known by your integrity. What kind of reputation are you leaving behind?

Related Passages: Acts 6:1-4; Phil 2:5-11

July 29

Reflecting At Independence Rock

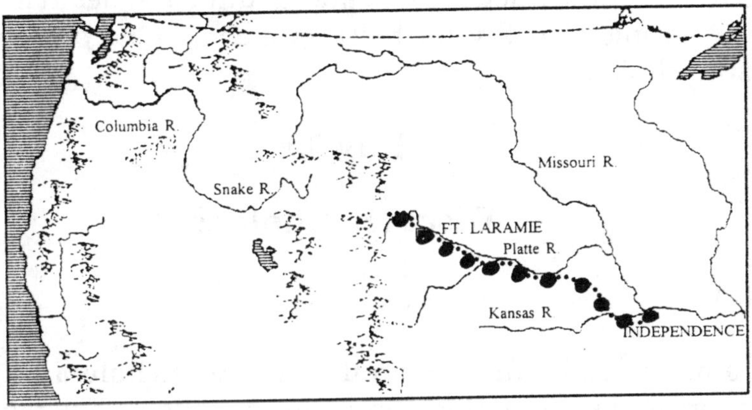

1843

Even though the emigrants didn't make it to Independence Rock on the "4th of July," they could still take time to celebrate how far they had come from Independence-815 miles. This Sunday was a good time to reflect on their "**Rock**" for the journey.

Today

The Psalms contain many references to Jesus being our "Rock" in various situtations. He is "my rock, my fortress and my deliverer."(18:2); ". . . my Rock and Redeemer."(19:14); ". . . He set my feet on a rock and gave me a firm place to stand."(40:2); ". . . lead me to the rock that is higher than I."(61:2); and ". . . He is my Rock, and there is no wickedness in Him."(92:15)The pioneers saw large rocks as **solid** and **unmovable**, something to count on as places of safety. We can also count on Jesus as a refuge in our lives. Is He your Rock?

Related Passages: Deut 32:4; Ps 18:1-3;
1 Pet 2:5,9

Death, Disease and Acts of Diety

Between Independence Rock and South Pass, death and disease became a reality for these pioneers. One pioneer was lost to cholera.

July 30

Disease: Cholera

1843

The most deadly disease on the Trail was **cholera**. Caused by consuming contaminated water or foods, cholera symptoms included vomiting, diarrhea, "(resulting) in dehydration, . . . shock and death." **55**

Today

Today we have the technology enabling us to understand the causes of many **diseases**. However, we are still susceptible to such maladies as the e-coli bacteria-caused by eating poorly cooked meat. How can we be healed of this and other diseases, such as cancer and heart disease?

Lesson On Healing Of Diseases

During Jesus' ministry He healed "**every** disease and sickness."(Matthew 4:23, 9:35) He gave the **same** power to His disciples.(Matthew 10:1) Jesus also promises us that we can do greater things than He did.(John 14:12) Thus His healing power is available to us today.

Related Passages: Ps 107:20; Prov 4:20-22
Matt 8:8

July 31

Disease: Mountain Fever

1843

The second most common disease on the Trail was "**mountain fever**"(today known as Rocky Mountain Spotted Fever or Colorado tick fever), since it was contracted west of Fort Laramie. Pierson Reading, one of the emigrants, succumbed to this disease, but eventually recovered. **56**

Today

Have you ever had a high fever, caused by a tick bite, virus or bacteria? A fever is the body's way of fighting disease. Thus the problem is not the fever; it is only the symptom. What is the **cause** of our many problems today?

Lesson On The Cause Of Our Problems

Jeremiah sees our sinful nature as the **root** cause of our individual and societal problems: "The heart is deceitful above all things and beyond cure. Who can understand it?"(17:9) The only cure is to have a "**heart transplant**" performed by the Master Physician, Jesus. When we ask Him to direct our lives, He will replace our natural desires with His, thus giving us the power to solve our problems from the **inside out**. We must first change our individual outlook before we can begin to really tackle society's problems. Where do you begin to solve problems- with yourself or by trying to change society? Jesus recommends the former approach. Change yourself first.

Related Passages: Rom 8:6-8; Gal 6:8
1 Pet 2:11

August 1

A "Lonely Grave"

1843

Burials on the journey seemed crude. The **graves** were usually dug right on the Trail, and the wagons passed over the burial site to keep the scent from attracting wolves. Burnett describes the scene for Payne, who died of cholera: "We buried him in the wild, shelterless plains, close to the new road we had made, and the funeral scene was most sorrowful and impressive. Mr. Garrison, a Methodist preacher . . . delivered a most touching and beautiful prayer at the lonely grave." **57**

Today

Funerals in America today seem elaborate by comparison. Many families, wanting to leave a **legacy**, will purchase an expensive casket, and go to extravagant lengths. Glowing eulogies will be given, regardless of the deceased's character. Should this be the focus at funerals?

Lesson On Funerals

Hebrews 9:27 puts death in perspective: "Just as man is destined to die once, and after that to face judgment." However, the born-again Christian will not face judgment, but will be **resurrected** as Christ was raised from the dead. Paul, in the "Great Resurrection Chapter"(I Corinthians 15), explains this hope of eternal life. Is this your hope?

Related Passages: Ps 98:2; Is 50:10
John 16:7-8; Acts 16:31

August 2

"Dry Bones"

1843

Despite the best efforts of the families to provide a decent **burial** for their deceased loved ones, the "call of the wild" took its course. Some of the bones were dug up by wolves, leaving a gruesome reminder for those who followed. Mercifully, the families probably never knew these "dry bones" were scattered on the desert floor behind them.

Today

Usually we only see actual human bones in the biology lab, where a skeleton may be studied. Those learning anatomy, such as doctors, must be familiar with this structure, in order to treat the human body. Will these bones ever come to life again?

Lesson On Bones Coming Alive

Ezekiel, in his vision, saw a valley of **dry bones**, and was asked by God, "Son of man, can these bones live?"(37:3) The rest of this vision describes the bones coming together, adding tendons, flesh, skin and finally breath.(vv. 4-14) Even though this passage refers to the "whole house of Israel" coming together(v. 11), our bones will also come together at the resurrection of the dead: "But each in his own turn: Christ, the firstfruits, then, when He comes, those who belong to Him."(I Corinthians 15:23). Because of Christ, we will **live** again!

Related Passages: Matt 23:27-28; 1 Cor 15:57
Titus 2:13

August 3

Devil's Gate

1843

Five miles west of Independence Rock the emigrants encountered **Devil's Gate.** At 6,000 feet elevation this eerie feature was a " narrow cleft-370 feet deep, 1,500 feet long and as narrow as 50 feet in some places-by which the Sweetwater River breaks through a ridge . . . It was a gloomy place , and violent also when the water was high, so that a satanic denomination seemed fitting." **58**

Today

Why do we name some natural features that appear **sinister** after the devil, even though these phenomenon were ultimately placed on earth by God? Yellowstone National Park has a hot springs called "Devil's Cauldron." Do you believe in a personal devil that "makes you do something bad?"

Lesson On The Devil

Just as the Bible postulates a personal God, so does it describe a real devil. He is described as, "Your enemy the devil(who) prowls around like a roaring lion looking for someone to devour.(I Peter 5: 8) We deal with the devil by first submitting ourselves to God, then **resisting** him, "and he will flee from you."(James 4:7) When the devil knocks with temptation, send Christ to the door.

Related Passages: Luke 8:11-15; Eph 4:25-32
1 John 3:4-9

August 4

Split Rock

1843

A little farther West, and off the Trail, was Split Rock, at 6,200 feet elevation. This granite formation was notched with a V at its top. It served as an unerring guide to follow for several days, similar to looking through a gun sight to make sure you were "on target."

Today

If you hunt or trap shoot, you know the importance of using a sight to locate your target or game. In addition to a reliable rifle, you need a steady hand to bring down a clay pigeon, deer or elk. You also need to keep your eyes on the **target.** On what do you keep your sights in today's world of temptations?

Lesson On Fixing Your Eyes

David declares that his eyes "are fixed on you, O Sovereign Lord; in You I take refuge-do not give me over to death."(Psalm 141:8) The writer of Hebrews commands us to "**fix** our eyes on Jesus, the author and perfector of our faith, who for the joy that was before Him endured the cross, scorning its shame, and sat down at the right hand of the throne of God."(12:2) Jesus, the only person on earth who lived a **perfect life**, is the only unerring guide through life. Is He your "pathfinder?"

Related Passages: Matt 6:22-33; 18:6-9
Luke 4:18;Rev 3:14-22

August 5

Reflecting In The Mountain Air

1843

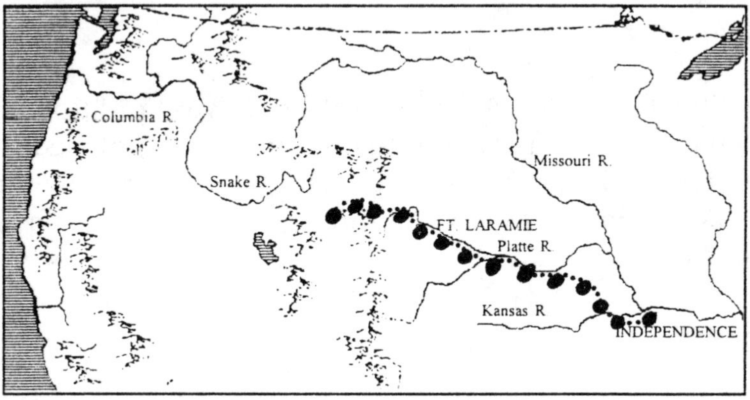

The emigrants found the **cool mountain air** to be therapeutic. The nightly freezing at these high elevations served to retard the spread of disease. Johnson exclaimed, ". . . the pure Mountain air and the rough wholesome manner of living have already restored many who were before feeble and afflicted to health, strength and activity . . . " **59**

Today

As you sit on the top of a **mountain** you have climbed, enjoying the cool breezes, reflect on the following questions:

1. Am I really happy, genuinely challenged and fulfilled in life?
2. In light of eternity, am I making a consistent investment For God's glory and His cause?
3. Is the direction my life is taking leading me toward a satisfying and meaningful future?
4. Can I honestly say that I am in the nucleus of God's will for me? **60**

Related Passages: Matt 5:14-16; Mark 16:15-20
John 14:12

South Pass

During this week the pioneers reached the contintental divide at South Pass, the halfway point of their journey, in present-day Wyoming.

August 6

Signs In The Heavens

1843

The emigrants experienced an unexplained **phenomenon**. William Newby wrote: "There was a very curious explosion at noon; first thare was some thing past over us in the element like a bowl of fier, then follwd it a long streek of blewsmoke in a zigzag form a bout 2 hundred yards long. Then followed it a very tremendious report as if it had bin large guns firing." **61** Was it a meteor or falling star?

Today

Have you ever seen something in the skies you couldn't identify. Was this rapdily moving **bright light** an alien spacecraft, a new comet, a UFO or a satellite? Whatever it was, your eyes followed it. How can God get our close and undivided attention?

Lesson On "Signs In The Heavens"

Jesus tells us during the last days signs that will occur in the **heavens**, ". . . the stars will fall from the sky . . ."(Matthew 24:29) "When these things began to take place, (we should) stand up and lift up(our) heads, because (our) redemption is drawing near."(Luke 21:28)

Related Passages: Gen 1:14-19; Exodus 7:1-6
Heb 2:1-4; Rev 13:13

August 7

The "Backbone Of North America"

1843

On this day the Oregon Emigrating Company reached South Pass, which Overton Johnson called the "**Backbone of North America.**" He describes the crossing: "both the ascent and descent were so gradual, had we not been told, we should have passed over the dividing ridge in the Rocky Mountains without knowing it. " **62**

Today

Have you crossed the Contintental Divide in the Western United States? Regardless of how steep the ascent or descent, the divide's summit marks a demarcation point. A river must flow either East or West-it can't flow in both directions. What have been significant **dividing points** in your life?

Lesson On Not Being Divided In Life

When Jesus healed the demon-possessed man(Matthew 12), he explained to the critical Pharisees that he couldn't be both Satan and God by explaining, "Every kingdom divided against itself will be ruined, and every city or household divided against itself will not stand."(v. 25) Jesus leaves no middle ground for the Christian: "He who is not with me is against me . . ."(v. 30) When we are on the "**divide of our life,**" we must choose either for or against Jesus. What is your choice?

Related Passages: Deut 8:11-14; Ps 44:20-21
Jer 6:16; 2 Pet 2:20-21

August 8

Highest Point On The Trail

1843

At approximately 7,500 feet elevation, South Pass marked the **highest point** on the Trail. While traveling 900 miles from Independence(800 feet elevation), the emigrants gradually gained 6,700 feet to this pass. The oxen pulling the wagons averaged an ascent of seven feet per mile.

Today

What is the highest elevation you have climbed, either by hiking, biking or automobile? Climbing to 14,000 feet on Long's Peak in Colorado has been the highest climb for this author. Still that is less than half the elevation of the world's highest mountain(Everest at 29,028 feet). Why do we try to reach **to the heavens**?

Lesson On Reaching To The Heavens

The Genesis account of the building of the **Tower of Babel**(11:1-9) explains men's motivation for this tower, "Come, let us build ourselves a city, with a tower that reaches to the heavens, so that we may **make a name for ourselves** . . ."(v. 4) This huge public works failed because God confuse(d) their language, so they would not understand each other(v. 7) God had a better idea. Instead of allowing man to reach Him by our own efforts, **He reached down to us** by sending His son for our redemption. Are you redeemed and elevated by God?

Related Passages: Zech 14:3-4; Matt 24:3-14
Heb 8:1-6

August 9

Most Important Landmark

1843

Even though South Pass was not a landmark in the sense of a towering natural feature, **symbolically** it was the **most important landmark** on the journey for two reasons: (1) this crossing marked the start of the frontier called the Oregon Territory, and (2) without this "low saddle" in the mountains, wheeled vehicles such as covered wagons could not have crossed the high Rockies and continued the Trail to Oregon.

Today

What are the most important "landmark accomplishments" in your life? Was it graduating from college? How about your marriage and having children? Was it "getting to the top" in your job? Was it moving to a new geographic area? What does **God see** as the most important accomplishments in your life?

Lesson On Important Events

God's value system is radically different than our societal beliefs. Whereas we reward working hard, God rewards our **faith**-and even gives it to us: "For it is by **grace** you have been saved, through **faith**-and this not from yourselves, it is the **gift of God**-not by works, so that no one can boast."(Ephesians 2:8,9) God rewards our dependence on Him. Have you surrendered completely to Him?

Related Passages: Jer 6:16; Matt 17:20; Rom 12:3
Heb 11:6

August 10

Seasons Of Life

1843

Even though the pioneers were traveling in a group to Oregon, many of the routine aspects of **life,** or **death,** went on. During this week a birth occurred, followed three days later by a death. "On August 6 John Pennington's wife gave birth to a daughter, and on the 9th a young man named Stevenson died of a fever contracted near Fort Laramie. **63** So it goes.

Today

What is your favorite season of the year? Is it spring, when the buds, leaves and flowers sprout? How about summer, with its outdoor activities? Maybe its autumn, with its colorful leaves and crisp evenings? And don't forget winter, with its pure snow and reflective indoor times?

Lesson On Seasons Of Life

Solomon lists the following activities of the pioneers and us today:(Ecclesiastes 3:1-7)

> "a time to be born and a time to die,
> a time to plant and a time to uproot,
> a time to kill and a time to heal,
> a time to tear down and a time to build,
> a time to weep and a time to laugh,
> a time to mourn and a time to dance,
> a time to scatter stones and a time to gather them,
> a time to embrace and a time to refrain,
> a time to search and a time to give up,
> a time to keep and a time to throw away,
> a time to tear and a time to mend,
> a time to be silent and a time to speak,
> a time to love and a time to hate, . . ."

Related Passages: Psalm 1:1-3; Prov 15:23
Gal 6:6-10

August 11

Halfway There!

1843

The Oregon Emigrating Company had now reached the **halfway point**-approximately 900 miles from Independence. From now on there would be no thought of turning back-no more "gobacks." Except for crossing the Blue Mountains in Oregon, the rest of the journey would be literally downhill. But they still had a long way to go to achieve their goal, and tough times still lay ahead. Westward Ho!

Today

Have you ever set out to achieve a goal, and stopped when you were only half completed? Did you receive any satisfaction from "having come this far?" How does this feeling of "**half an accomplishment**" compare to having completed your goal? Is it better to not have started a project than to begin and not finish it? Do you have "half-climbed mountains" in your life?

Lesson On Being Lukewarm

Jesus warns the Church about being lukewarm: "I know your deeds, that you are neither cold nor hot. I wish you were either one or the other! So, because you are **lukewarm**-neither cold nor hot-I am about to spit you out of my mouth."(Revelation 3:15-16) Jesus wants us to be a "**hot Christian:**" "So whether you eat or drink, or whatever you do, do it all for the glory of God."(I Corintians 10:31) Are you hot, cold or lukewarm? Be hot!

Related Passages: Neh 8:10; Dan 10:19
Eph 3:16-17; Col 1:10-12

August 12

Enjoying Family Time

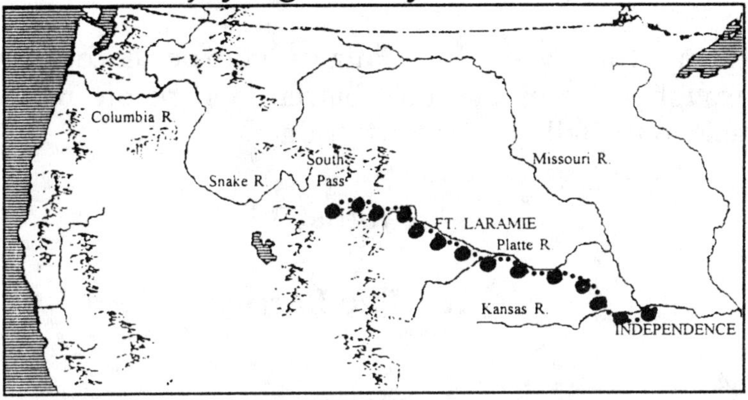

1843

Even though the families traveled together, they probably didn't spend "**quality time**" with each other during the week. Men, women and children each performed their assigned duties. Therefore a Sunday rest day was a good time for families to enjoy each other by playing games, visiting, reading, picking flowers or taking exploratory walks.

Today

Do you set aside a **family time** once a week? If you do, what types of topics do you discuss? Moses commands us to talk about God's commandments: "Love the Lord your God with all your **heart** and with all your **soul** and with all your **strength.** These commandments that I give you today are to be upon your hearts. Impress them on your children. Talk about them when you sit at home and when you walk along the road, when you lie down and when you get up."(Deuteronomy 6:5-7) We should make talking about what God requires of us a natural part of each day, not just on Sunday in church. Is God a natural part of your family's conversation each day of the week?

Related Passages: Amos 3:3; John 8:12
Eph 3:14-20

Fort Bridger

During this week the emigrants experienced traveling through some of the most barren land before reaching an **oasis** in the wilderness-Fort Bridger.

August 13

It's The Berries!

1843

Near Pacific Springs the ladies gathered a special dietary **treat.** Sara Jane Hill writes, ". . . we found plenty of blue gooseberries maybe you think it wasn't a treat, every women and child was out with its bucket or cup. We had some of the finest dumplings for dinner you ever seen in your life." **64**

Today

Have you ever gathered **edible berries** or fruits from bushes or trees? What if all of a sudden these plants only produced leaves, and gave no more lucious fruit?

Lesson Of The Fig Tree

Jesus, as a lesson, commands the fig tree to "never bear fruit again," and uses this withered tree to illustrate that-with **faith** and no doubting-the disciples could do this and also "move mountains."(Matthew 21:18-22) Do you have this type of faith?

Related Passages: Matt 7:15-20; John 15:1-8
Heb 13:15-17

August 14

The Desert

1843

Through most of present day Wyoming, the emigrants were traveling through **desert** country. John Shively describes the desert: "The glare of the sun on the desert is sickening. No water for many miles . . ." **65**

Today

Have you traveled through desert country, especially in the American West and Southwest? Did you see it as **dry,** desolate and devoid of much life, or as a place of pristine **beauty** with colorful tones? Many times the desert is used as a symbol of isolation, reflection, waiting and testing of our souls. Wilderness experiences can be valuable.

Lesson On The Desert Experience

Chapters 2,3 and 4 of Exodus describe Moses' 40 year "desert experience." It was not until the burning bush experience(Chapter 3) that God told Moses to "bring my people the Israelites out of Egypt."(3:10) As God did with Moses, so He does with us: He peels "away our masks so that we may discover who we really are. . . It is at this stage of nakedness that the Lord performs some of His best refining work in our lives." **66** Through this **training period**, Moses came back to his people ready to be a leader. Have you gone through your refining "desert experience.?"

Related Passages: Deut 4:22-24; Matt 4:1-11
Js 4:7-10

August 15

Mirage

1843

John Shively describes his desert experience: ". . . but on looking around you see a lake or river on your right or left. It is not far to the lake. Off I go. I get no nearer the lake. It is a **mirage** caused by the glare of the sun through the dry atmosphere on parched earth." **67** Even the animals tried to drink this imaginary water.

Today

Have you ever seen a mirage in the desert? How about driving down the pavement on a hot summer day, seemingly seeing what looks like a recent rain? In either case, you are deceived to find that when you arrive at the true scene, your **distorted image** is not real. How else are we deceived by wrong perceptions today?

Lesson On Being Deceived

In Matthew 24 Jesus warns that one of the signs of the end of the age is that "many will come in My name, claiming, 'I am the Christ,' and will deceive many(v 5); . . . and many **false prophets** will appear and deceive many people"(v 11); and these false Christs and prophets "will appear and perform great signs and miracles to deceive even the elect-if that were possible"(v 24). The best way to avoid following a counterfeit Jesus is to know the **real One**, by spending time with Him. Have you developed this type of genuine relationship?

Related Passages: John 6:47; 2 Cor 5:17;
1 John 4:14

August 16

Dryness

1843

The desert heat and dryness also caused a problem for the emigrants' **wagon wheels**. The wooden wheels were crafted in the humid Midwest. Now in this low humidity, the wooden wheels shrunk from the iron tires, causing them to fall off. The temporary solution was to tighten the loose tire by driving wedges between it and the wheel. **68** The permanent solution needed a blacksmith to refit the iron wheel.

Today

Have you moved from the more humid East or Midwest to the less humid Western United States? In addition to enjoying the cooler and bugless evenings, did you notice the increased **dryness** of your skin, or the drier finish on your furniture? The pioneers didn't have any chapstick or lotion for their skin. There is also another type of dryness.

Lesson On Dryness

When David was in the Desert of Judah, he used the metaphor of thirsting for God: ". . . my soul **thirsts** for you, my body longs for you, in a dry and weary land where there is no water."(Psalms 63:1) Thus we can seek and find God through our desert experiences, when we seek Him with **all our heart**.(Jeremiah 29:13) Are you on this kind of thirsty quest?

Related Passages: Ps 103:11-14; Is 35:5-10
Acts 3:19-21

August 17

Supplying At Fort Bridger

1843

Mountain men Jim Bridger and Louis Vasquez founded and built Fort Bridger just in time to **sell supplies** to the Oregon Emigrating Company. Mr. Bridger describes his fort: "I have established a small fort, with a blacksmith shop and a supply of iron in the road of the emigrants on Black's Fork of the Green River, which promises fairly . In coming out they are generally well supplied with money, but by the time they get here they are in need of all kinds of supples, horses, provision, smithwork, etc."**69**

Today

Yesterday's **trading posts** are like today's **malls.** Both are situated close to the main artery of travel, whether a trail or an interstate. They both provide one-stop shopping, offering an abundance of goods. How should the emigrants-and you-spend money for supplies?

Lesson On Spending Our Money

Even though Paul warns us that it is not wrong to be wealthy, it is"the **love of money** that is the root of all evil."(I Timothy 6:10) Jesus further warns us that we can't "serve two masters. . . You cannot serve both God and money."(Matthew 6:24) The question is: "Are you serving your wealth, or is your wealth serving God?" Which is it for you?

Related Passages: Is 55:2-5; Matt 25:14-30
Acts 8:18-25; 2 Tim 3:1-7

August 18

Women At The Fort

1843

When women rested in small groups, the handwork came out of their pockets, wagons and trunks. **Conversation** flowed freely and chatting continued merrily throughout the day-making idle time pass quickly and bonding the women together.

Today

There is nothing so binding as time spent together with a **joint project**. Quilting bees, cross-stitich clubs and handiwork magazines abound. Little has changed our need to share troubles, goals, and solutions. An embroidered handerkerchief appears, a needlepoint chair cover or knitted shawl emerges from a sewing bag and the parlor conversation begins as it has for hundreds of years-women bonded over the art of sharing their lives through conversation over needlework.

Lesson On Women's Handwork

Workers were sought to complete the grandeur of the Temple. The best fabrics and silk were woven into lush **tapestries** for the curtains(Exodus 26:36). Dorcas was known throughout the region for her expert sewing and keen eye for stitched fabrics(Acts 9: 39). How often we need to remember the age-old art of needlework and the deep satisfaction it brings to the soul of the sower. How are women bonded today?

Related Passages: Prov 24,31; Matt 19:23-30
Luke 24:13-27; John 15:5-8

August 19

Conversing On The Sabbath

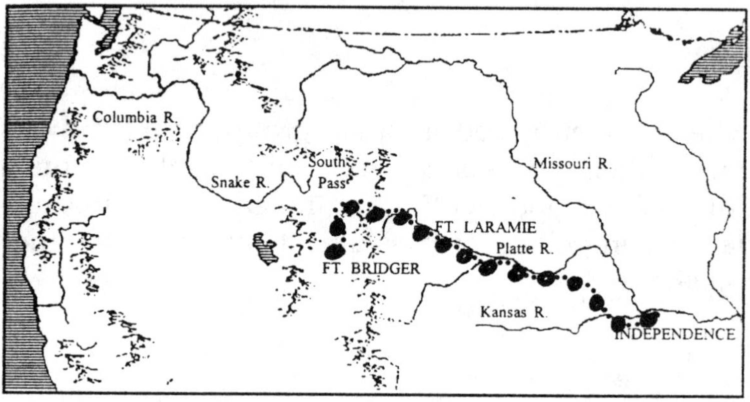

1843

Women have long sought the deep satisfaction of sewing, and men the keen need of sharing political viewpoints, and working with their hands. Life then as now proves no different in the seeking of peace on the Sabbath, and in sharing what brings restful joy. Ladies left the dusty road and bumpy wagons to enjoy company, and brought civility to the trail life with stitches into calico cotton. Men shared wagon repair stories, wondered aloud about their westward choices and planned ahead for better days with their families. Sabbaths then and now were meant for **meaningful relationships**, shared meals, easy talk and bringing perspective to the daily grinds of workday walks and bygone weeks.

Today

Application: Jesus also took time to **share** with his disciples when he needed to rest, share prayers, talk about His goals and the journey.(Mark 3:7) May we also keep these times of knowing ourselves, appreciating others and praising our wonderful God.

Related Passages: Prov 18:24; Phil 4:6-9
Col 3:15; Heb 13:5

The Bear River Valley

After traveling through the dry and dusty desert, the emigrants finally enjoyed the fresh **water** and green **grass** of the Bear River Valley, in the present states of Idaho and Utah.

August 20

The Lush And Beautiful Valley

1843

Overton Johnson described the **Bear River Valley** "as one to eight miles wide with good soil, excellent grass, and flax that grew spontaneously . . .a sparsity of trees, only a few cottonwoods scattered along the river." **70**

Today

Valleys provide a **colorful beauty** all their own. The small farms, with their green fields of corn, beans, or potatoes, contrast with the golds of wheat, oats or hay. Cattle, horses or sheep graze contently beside a meandering stream on the valley floor near shady trees.

Lesson On Peaceful Valleys

The well-known 23rd Psalm paints this same picture: "He makes me lie down in green pastures, He leads me beside the still waters."(v. 2) Are you enjoying your quiet lush times with the Lord?

Related Passages: Ps 103:2-4; Is 26:3
John 14:27

August 21

Catching Fish

1843

Finally a chance to catch and eat fresh trout-a new species that existed only west of the Rockies. Overton Johnson explains: "These streams abound with a fine fish called the **Mountain Trout**." **71** Since there was no more buffalo for fresh meat, these fish provided a welcome variety to their monotonous diet.

Today

Have you ever fished for-and caught-trout? Did you fly-fish, or use a regular rod and reel? What type of bait did you use-night crawlers, salmon eggs, corn, or artificial bait? Did you fish from the shore, use a float or a boat? Regardless of your methodology, your objective was the same-to catch fish. How else can we "go fishing?"

Lesson On Catching Fish

Jesus knew how to catch fish-literally and figuratively. After His disciples had fished all night-and caught nothing-Jesus commanded them to, "Throw your net on the right side of the boat and you will find some."(John 21: 6) They did indeed find some-153 fish in all!(v.11) More importantly, Jesus called His disciples-some of whom were fishermen-to "Come, follow me, . . . and I will make you **fishers of men.**"(Matthew 4:19; Mark 1:17) What kind of fish are you catching?

Related Passages: Ps 37:4; 107:9; Joel 2:26
Matt 5:6

August 22

"An Air Of Quiet Security"

1843

John C. Fremont described the following idyllic pioneer camping scene in the Bear River Valley: ". . . The edge of the wood . . . was dotted with the white covers of emigrant wagons . . . where the smokes were rising lazily from the fires, around which the women were occupied in preparing the evening meal, and the children playing in the grass; and the herds of cattle grazing about in the bottom, had an **air of quiet security,** and civilized comfort, that made a rare sight for the traveller in such a remote wilderness." **72**

Today

What types of settings make you feel **secure**? Is it a strong family, that prays and plays together? Is it a well-paying job, with seniority? Is it living in a house, and having an automobile, with security systems? Is it accumulating a comfortable retirement? From where does our real **security** come?

Lesson On Security

David's secret to security was to "set the Lord always before (him). Because (God) is at his right hand, David would "not be shaken." David's response is a glad heart, a rejoicing tongue; and a body that "will rest secure."(Psalm 16: 8.9) Is this where your security lies, in God who is before you?

Related Passages: Ps 63:5-6; Is 55:2; 58:10-11
John 6:35

August 23

The "Pathfinder"

1843

Captain **John C. Fremont**, who mapped the Trail in 1842 as far as South Pass, was sent the next year by the US Army to map the entire route. Convinced that another feasible route farther south did not exist for the wagon trains, Fremont's party caught up with the Great Migration at the Bear River Valley. Later this same year his party reached the Columbia River. His maps and descriptions proved valuable for future journeys to Oregon.

Today

When traveling today, we have many routes that will lead to the same destination. How do we know which one to take? Do we consult AAA, or, with maps and atlantes, figure the route ourself? Do we choose the most frequently traveled interstate, or "the road less traveled?" as Robert Frost did in his famous poem, "The Road Not Taken." **73** How do you know what is the "**right path**" for your life?

Lesson On Choosing "The Right Path"

The first step in choosing the right path is to **ask the Lord** to show us His ways, and to teach us His path.(Psalm 25:4), so that "we may walk in His paths."(Isaiah 2:3 and Micah 4:2) "The path of the righteous is level . . .(Isaiah 26:7) and straight(Psalm 27:11 and Proverbs 3:6) Are you on the "right path?" Where is your "journey" leading you?

Related Passages: Mark 11:24; John 16:23-24
Eph 1:3

August 24

Joyfulness

1843

By now the Oregon Emigrating Company had traveled nearly 1,200 miles to the "promised land." They had overcome many trials, relating to weather(too much rain, intense heat, dust and dryness), accidents, disease, and even death. Beneath these adverse cirumstances, they could still be joyful, particularly when working together through the beautiful Bear River Valley .

Today

What is the difference between **happiness** and **joyfulness**? While happiness is temporarily related to pleasant events(parties, good news, etc.), joy is more lasting and deep-seated, and is independent of circumstances? How can we be joyful, regardless of our situation?

Lesson On Joyfulness

The Old Testament prophet Habakkuk resolves that, even though his crops fail, his "fields produce no food," and he has no livestock, he "will rejoice in the Lord, (he) will be joyful in God my Savior."(3:17-18) Jesus promises His children **joy**, both on this earth, and in eternity with Him. If we have an intimate relationship with Him(John 15:5), His "joy may be in us and that (our) joy may be complete."(John 15:11) Do you have this fulfilling joy?

Related Passages: Is 58:10-11; Rom 12:9-13
1 Thess 5:14-22

August 25

Marriages On The Trail

1843

Boys and girls, and men and women probably **courted** each other along the Trail. If they became serious, marriage could be the result. All they had to do was find a minister. The wedding ceremony would not be elaborate, but they could fashion a ring and pick flowers. They had plenty of wilderness witnesses.

Today

Do you remember the courtship and love leading to your marriage? Was your **wedding** a gala event, a private ceremony or did you elope? What have been the must important factors keeping your marriage strong and together? What advice does the Bible give?

Lesson On Strong Marriages

Ephesians 5: 21-33 and I Peter 3:1-7 give **practical advice** to husbands and wives. Paul draws an analogy between Christ and the Church, and husbands and wives. As Christ loved and gave Himself to the Church, husbands should do the same for their wives(v.25). As the Church submits to Christ, so should wives **submit** to their husbands(v.24). Both should submit to one another out of reverence for Christ(v.21). Peter encourages wives to be submissive to their husbands(v.1), while husbands should be considerate of their wives(v.7). Is your marriage based on these **Biblical principles**?

Related Passages: Josh 24:15; Eph 4:31-32
1 Pet 3:1-11

August 26

Reflecting Around The Campfire

1843

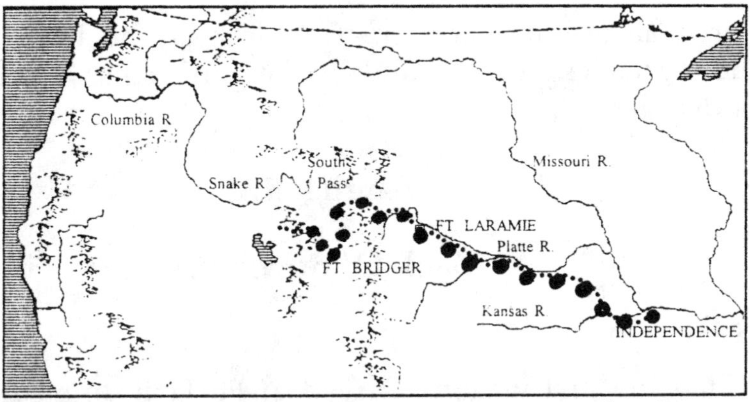

Campfires served more than utilitarian purposes for the pioneers. In addition to providing fuel for cooking and washing dishes, and warmth at night, gathering around the blazing fire became a time for intimate conversation. There's something special about staring into the **crackling bonfire** at night, causing you to share your innermost deep thoughts and feelings. You focus on the fire and not on each other. Maybe that's why you feel more free to share and dream in this setting.

Today

Have you shared your spiritual journey with someone else around an evening campfire? Have you felt closer to God in this setting? This can be a time for you to share **wisdom** from the Holy Spirit with your campfire partner. Paul says. "We(committed Christians) have not received the spirit of the world but the Spirit who is from God, that we may understand what God has freely given us."(I Corinthians 2: 12) Do you have this wisdom that comes directly from the Holy Spirit? Have you shared it?

Related Passages: Is 44:3; John 16:7-8
Acts 11:4; 2 Pet 3:9

Fort Hall

Fort Hall was the most crucial place on the Trail. Would they "**go back**," or "**beyond**" to Oregon? This was the week of decision.

August 27

Back O' Beyond?

1843

Today the first wagons arrived at Ft. Hall. Immediately a debate ensued: "Could our wagons go beyond Ft. Hall(as none had gone before), or do we have to leave our wagons at the fort, and switch to pack animals, as had been done previously?" Peter Burnett advised the latter method, but Marcus Whitman "encouraged and aided us with every means in his power" to keep the **wagons rolling. 74** Most thankfully followed Whitman's advice!

Today

The authors have also gone **beyond** by giving up secure jobs to create **Back O' Beyond Victorian Bed and Breakfast**, on the Oregon Trail near Ft. Hall in Pocatello, Idaho.

Lesson On Going Back or Beyond?

Jeremiah encouraged the Israelites to , "Stand at the crossroads(Jerusalem) and look; ask for the ancient paths, ask where the good way is, and walk in it, and you will find rest for your souls."(6:16) Have you gone beyond to a **higher level** in your walk with Christ?

Related Passages: Deut 30:19-20; Josh 24:14-15
Heb 11:23-26

August 28

"Roll A Rock In Your Garden"

1843

Nathaniel Wyeth, a New Englander who built Fort Hall in 1834, was dogged by misfortunes and competition while establishing his trading post on the Snake River. His supply ship sank before arriving in the Oregon Territory. Then his contract to supply trappers in exchange for their pelts was abrogated by an established trading firm. He vowed to get even by declaring, "you think you have your own little Eden out here but I am going to **roll a rock** into your garden." **75**

Today

Have you ever experienced one **misfortune** after another- sickness, death, divorce, loss of a job? You realize life is "not a bed of roses," but too many bad things at a time cause you to doubt yourself and God. You ask, "God, why don't you roll away my stones?"

Lesson On "Rolling Away Stones"

The three women in Mark 16 were facing an obstacle in their lives. Coming to the tomb to anoint Jesus' body after His death, they asked each other, "Who will roll the stone away from the entrance of the tomb?"(v.3) Their question was unnecessary because . . . "when they looked up, they saw that the stone, which was very large, had been rolled away."(v.4) Jesus can **roll your "stones" away**, sometimes before they are even a problem!

Related Passages: John 11:38-44; 1 Pet 2: 4-10
Rev 2:17

August 29

Hospitality At The Fort

1843

Finally succumbing to a more powerful competitor, Mr. Wyeth sold out to the British Hudson's Bay Company. The Chief Factor at Fort Hall, Richard Grant, treated the Americans with "kindness and **hospitality** . . . (that is) almost extreme, and it appears to give him much pleasure to have it in his power to serve them." **76**

Today

Do you have the gift of hospitality? When people enter your house, do you have the ability to make them feel **comfortable** and "at home?" One of the authors(Sherrie) definitely does. Just ask the people who have stayed at Back O' Beyond Bed and Breakfast! What does the Bible say about this God-given gift to make people feel at ease?

Lesson On Practicing Hospitality

Paul enjoyed receiving the gift of hospitality. After his shipwreck, he was washed ashore on the island of Malta. "There was an estate nearby that belonged to Publius, the chief official of the island. He welcomed us to his home for three days entertaining us **hospitably**."(Acts 28:7) Paul also commands us to, "Share with God's people who are in need. Practice hospitality."(Romans 12:13) Peter asks us to, "Offer hospitality to one another without grumbling."(I Peter 4:9) Is this your gift?

Related Passages: John 2:1-12; 1 Tim 6:17-19
Heb 13:16

August 30

Anger At The Fort

1843

With a paucity of supplies at the fort, the late-arriving imigrants found the **supplies** nearly exhausted. Chief Factor Grant, who was seen as hospitable by the early-arrivals, angered the later group bound for California. Two men from that train threatened the commander with violence if he refused to sell them part of the supplies he had held back for his own personnel. **77**

Today

What happens today when essential supplies become low? Do you remember the long gas lines during the Arab oil boycott of the 1970s? There were instances of people getting angry and threatening violence to someone who tried to cut in line. **Anger** and abuse in our families are all too common today. What can be done about breaking this cycle?

Lesson On Anger and Forgiveness

Solomon advises us to turn anger away by giving "a gentle answer."(Proverbs15:1) Paul cautions us, "In your **anger do not sin**; Do not let the sun go down while you are still angry."(Ephesians 4:26) Paul concludes that love "is **not easily angered**."(I Corinthians 13:5) James wants, "Everyone (to be) quick to listen, slow to speak and slow to become **angry**."(1:19) It's tough to control your anger yourself. That's where Christ's practical love helps.

Related Passages: Neh 9:17; Is 48:9-11
Luke 11:1-4

August 31

Widowed At The Fort

1843

The Oregon Emigrating Company lost another emigrant. Daniel Richardson of Franklin County, Missouri, died on this day at Ft. Hall. He left his wife and two children to continue without him. **78** Another widow on the Trail.

Today

How many **widows** do you know in your community? With the average lifespan of men being less than for women, more and more women are left by themselves in their homes. Who takes care of these widows-usually in their old age-perhaps the family if they live close by; friends or the nursing home staff can help? Who else can assist them in their need?

Lesson On Taking Care of Widows

Twice in the Psalms David sees the Lord as taking care of widows. He is "a **defender** of widows . . ."(68:5). He "**sustains** . . . the widow."(146:9) Timothy has this advice for caring for widows: "Give proper **recognition** to those widows who are really in need. But if a widow has children or grandchildren, these should learn first of all to put their religion into practice by caring for their own family and so repaying their parents and grandparents, for this is pleasing to God."(I Timothy 5:3,4) Finally, James says "pure and faultless" religion "is this: to look after orpans and widows in their distress . . ."(1:27)

Related Passages: Deut 10:12-14; Is 1:16-17
Luke 2:36-38

September 1

Inflexible Determination

1843

The emigrants had now trekked over 1,200 miles from Independence, just about two-thirds of the way to Oregon City. Even though they were about to travel over some of the most difficult country of the entire journey, Peter Burnett summed up the pioneers **resolution**, "We fully comprehended the situation, but we never faltered in our inflexible determination to accomplish this trip." **79**

Today

You've probably heard of the locker room saying, "When the going gets tough, the tough gets going." How do you respond to a challenge-do you overcome or succumb? You can't accomplish a particularly difficult task until you first determine in your mind that you will bring it to completion. How does **bold determination** fit into the Christian life?

Lesson On Determination

Jesus and Paul were both very determined. Even though Jesus knew He would die for us, "As the time approached for Him to be taken up to heaven, Jesus resolutely set out for Jerusalem."(Luke 9:51) Paul summed up his life proclaiming, "I have fought the good fight, I have finished the race, I have kept the faith."(II Timothy 4:7) Will we be able to echo Paul's words near the end of our life?

Related Passages: Ruth 1:16-18; Luke 22:20-23
1 Cor 2:1-5

September 2

Sunday School

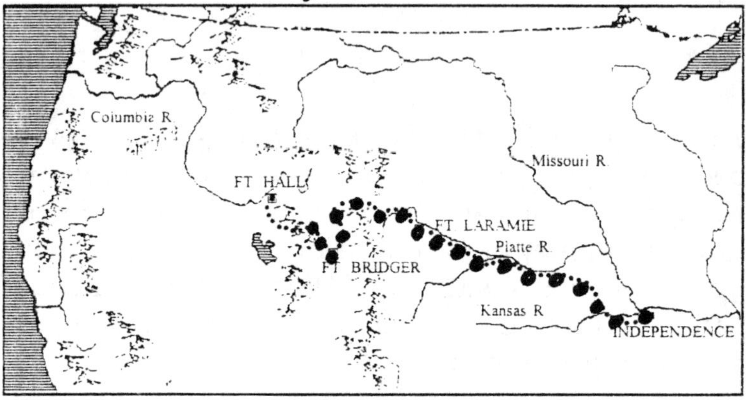

1843

What kind of an education did the children receive along the Trail? If they were "back in civilization," they would be attending a one-room school with a regular teacher. Now they may have been "**home-schooled**" in their covered wagon. Probably Sunday was the only time the parents had for this instruction. They may have also taught Bible lessons to their children on the Lord's Day.

Today

There has been a resurgence of home schooling today. In this setting parents have the freedom to teach the **cognitive, moral** and **spiritual** values they deem important to their children. They can also tutor and mentor their children on an individual basis in their own home. Jesus, as a boy, learned from mentors. He spent time "in the temple courts, sitting among the teachers, listening to them and asking them questions."(Luke 2:46) When Jesus' parents finally found Him after three days, they didn't understand that He "had to be in His father's house."(Luke 2:49) Are you bringing up your children in God's house?

Related Passages: Prov 1:5; Rom 15:1-6
1 Cor 4:6-7

First Wagons West

During this week the Oregon Emigrating Company made history. They were the first emigrant wagons to travel **beyond** Fort Hall.

September 3

Breaking New Trails

1843

With each mile the emigrants advanced West, they confounded the naysayers who said taking wagons all the way to the Willamette Valley could **not** be done. "That is the true spirit of pioneering, breaking new trails and doing what others less determined would not attempt." **80**

Today

History recounts examples of pioneers in various fields of endeavor. Remember the Wright brothers, who heard, "It will never fly, Wilbur." That was before the first airplane flight at Kitty Hawk, North Carolina, in 1903. How can we "**soar to new heights**" today?

Lesson On Traveling Beyond

Habakkuk sees "The Sovereign Lord (as) my strength; He makes my feet like the feet of a deer, He enables me to go on the heights."(3:19) We can reach a **higher level** as we continually **yield** to Christ's power.

Related Passages: Is 41:10; Acts 2
Heb 10:24-25

September 4

Friendship

1843

Since the pioneers worked, walked and lived together during their journey, there was ample time to develop **friendships**. "One of the most common means of interaction along the Trail was the spontaneous visits among the wagons . . . This face-to-face communication usually occurred at mealtimes, nights or on rest days" **81**

Today

How important is **cultivating relationships** with friends and neighbors to you? Do you take the time to get to know their interests and needs? Aristotle saw friendship as essential: "For without friends no one would choose to live, though he had all other goods . . . for with friends men are more able both to think and to act. . . for no one would choose the whole world on condition of being alone, since man is a political creature and one whose nature is to live with others." **82**

Lesson On Cultivating Friendships

Solomon sees the value of friendship when he concludes: "Two are better than one, because they have a good return for their work: If one falls down, his friend can help him up."(Ecclesiastes 4:9) Paul encourages us to, "Carry each other's **burdens,** and in this way you will fulfill the law of Christ."(Galatians 6:2) What burdens of friends are you carrying?

Related Passages: Rom 15:5-7; Col 3:16
Eph 2:19,22; 1 John 1:3,7

September 5

From Friendship To Intimacy

1843

The Oregon Emigrating Company was composed of over 900 persons. Along the way new acquaintances and **friendships** were made. Of these friendships, there were probably only a few that developed into intimate relationships.

Today

You probably have many acquaintances and friendships, but with how many persons do you share the **deepest** aspects of your life? Aristotle sees true friendship as selective: "One cannot be a friend to many people in the sense of having friendship of the perfect type with them, just as one cannot be in love with many people at once . . . Therefore friends in excess of those who are sufficient for our own life are superfluous." **83** When do friendships become intimate?

Lesson On Intimacy

Solomon sees **intimacy** in the context of stimulating discussions: "As iron sharpens iron, so one man sharpens another."(Proverbs 27:17) An example of an intimate friendship between David and Jonathan is recounted in I Samuel 18. ". . . Jonathan became **one in spirit** with David."(v.1) "And Jonathan made a covenant with David because he loved him as himself."(v.3) Do you have this type of intimate friendship with another person?

Related Passages: Prov 18:24; John 15:9-17
Js 2:23-24

September 6

Morning And Sunrise On The Trail

1843

Since the pioneers were early risers, they saw many beautiful **sunrises.** Jesse Applegate's "A Day With The Cow Column of 1843" gives an hourly glimpse of the morning duties. "It is four o'clock A.M.; the sentinels on duty have discharged their rifles-the signal that the hours of sleep are over. . . by 5 o'clock the herders begin to contract the great, moving circle(of livestock) . . . From 6 to 7 o'clock . . . breakfast is to be eaten, the tents struck, the wagons loaded and the teams yoked . . . at 7 o'clock, the signal to march sounds . . . " **84**

Today

Are you a morning person, like a **lark**, who enjoys arising early to greet the sunrise? Do you have your "quiet time" during the solitude of the breaking dawn?

Lesson On Enjoying The Early Morning

Two Old Testament prophets relate God's characteristics to the morning, and its beautiful sunrises. Habakkuk describes God's splendor "like the sunrise."(3:4) Jeremiah relates God's love and compassion: "Because of the Lord's great love we are not consumed, for his compassions never fail. They are new every morning; great is Your faithfulness." (Lamentations 3:22-23) Do you worship God's attributes, from the sun to the **Son**, this way?

Related Passages: Josh 10:12-13; Is 38:4-8
Matt 5:43-48

September 7

Evening And Sunset On The Trail

1843

After supper a more relaxed atmosphere prevailed, with a chance to enjoy the purple, yellow and pink **sunsets**. Applegate continues: "It is not yet 8 o'clock when the first watch is to be set . . . a violin makes lovely music . . . in another quarter a flute gives its mellow and melancholy notes to the still night air . . . All is hushed and reposed from the fatigue of the day, save the vigilant guard . . . " **85**

Today

Night can be seen as either a positive or a negative time for you. Are you a "**night owl**", enjoying the late hours? Is this when you are the most creative? Before **nightfall** do you also take time to enjoy the "alpenglow" of a golden sunset behind the mountains, or the sun's reflection on the ocean? Or do you see the night as ominous and foreboding, afraid and wondering what's out there?

Lesson On Enjoying The Nightime Hours

The Bible sees **songs** as important in the night. Elihu, one of Job's friends, sees God "who gives songs in the night."(Job 35:10) In the Psalms David sees the Lord's song with him at night.(42:8) He also "remembered (His) "songs in the night."(77:6) "(We) will not fear the terror of night . . ."(91:5) With God's presence, we can enjoy the darkness. Do you?

Related Passages: Joel 2:10-11; Luke 23:44-49
Eph 4:25-32; Rev 21:22-27

September 8

Rainbow In The Sky

1843

A **rainbow** is a rarity, especially in the desert. With so little rain, it must have been an awesome sight to see this colorful phenomenon in the Western sky. No doubt these pioneers looked for the proverbial "pot of gold" at the end of the rainbow, which to them was the fertile Willamette Valley.

Today

Do you remember the times you have seen a rainbow? Do you remember the colors? The name ROY G BIV will assist you-red, orange, yellow, green, blue, indigo and violet, in that order. A rainbow is always a **refreshing sign**, since the rain has ceased, and the sun is breaking from the clouds, signaling a brighter day. The Bible even makes references to a rainbow, and "brighter days" to come.

Lesson On A Rainbow

After the Great Flood, Genesis 6-8, God gave a covenant to Noah and his sons. "I have set my **rainbow** in the clouds, and it will be a sign of the covenant between Me and the earth. Whenever I bring clouds over the earth and the **rainbow** appears in the clouds, I will remember My **covenant** between Me and you and all living creatures of every kind. Never again will the waters become a flood to destroy all life."(Genesis 9:13-15) Just one of God's many promises for us!

Related Passages: Hos 10:12; 2 Pet 3:1-9
Rev 4:2-5

September 9

Enjoying The Stillness

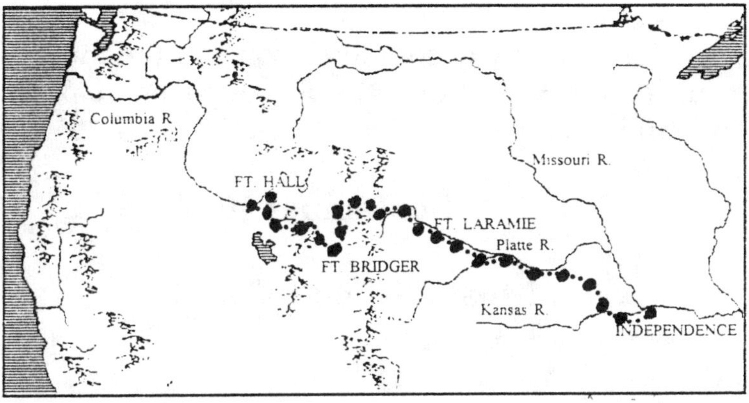

1843

When the wagons were moving, there were definite sounds along the Trail-the creaking of the wagons, the loud commands to the oxen, talking among the emigrants, the crack of the bullwhips, the mooing of the cattle, and the sharp rifle fire signaling the time to arise and to march. With the wagon train resting on Sunday, these sounds were minimized, allowing a **quieter** and gentler time of reflection.

Today

Do the modern urban noises drain your energy, and distract your attention from contemplative pursuits? Are they leaving you spiritually insensitive, a business-as-usual attitude toward the church you attend, the Bible study you used to enjoy or your prayer life? Maybe its time for "the **therapy of stillness**." **86** David commanded us to, "Be still and know that I am God."(Psalm 46:10) Elijah heard the Lord's voice, not in the wind, the earthquake, nor in the fire, but in "a **gentle whisper**."(I Kings 19:11-13) Do you hear God's voice speaking quietly to you?

Related Passages: Is 30:15; 32:16-20; 1 Thess 4:9-12
1 Pet 3:1-6

The Snake River Plateau

The emigrants now encountered some of the **most difficult terrain** of the trip, along the Snake River in present day Southern Idaho.

September 10

Most Difficult Country

1843

Theodore Talbot described this country: "We camped for the night on a high basaltic cliff overhanging the river and some two hundred and eighty feet above it. To reach the water we have to follow a path nearly a mile long winding down the face of the cliffs to the River side." **87**

Today

The authors live along the eastern end of the Snake River Plain, with their inaccessible steep cliffs. Even motorcyclist daredevil Evil Knivel couldn't jump the Snake River canyon near Twin Falls! How do you react to **trials** and **difficulties**?

Lesson On Difficulties

Paul says, ". . . for Christ's sake, I delight in weaknesses, in insults, in hardships, in persecutions, in **difficulties**. For when I am weak, then I am **strong**."(2 Corinthians 12:10) Have you experienced this paradox of power?

Related Passages: Matt 10:34-39; Rom 8:26-30
Gal 6:6-10

September 11

California Cutoff

1843

About fifty miles west of Fort Hall, some emigrants had to make an important **decision**-whether to cross the Raft River on the way to California, or whether to continue to follow the Snake River to Oregon. 38 emigrants choose the former route, while the vast majority(875) continued to Oregon. **88**

Today

Before starting a trip today you generally have a **destination** in mind. Have you ever changed course "in the middle of the stream?" While traveling you may have heard about a new place that you thought was more exciting or interesting. However, you may have found out the original route was the best one for you. Has this happened to you on your spiritual "journey" as well?

Lesson On Taking Cutoffs

Jesus makes two dogmatic statements about taking only **one road** that leads to life. In John He declares, "I am the way and the truth and the life. No one comes to the Father except by Me."(14:6) In Matthew, Jesus cautions, "Enter through the narrow gate. For wide is the gate and broad is the road that leads to destruction, and many enter through it. But small is the gate and narrow the road that leads to life, and only a few find it."(Matthew 7:13) **Jesus** is only one way!

Related Passages: Ps 119:25-32; Is 66:1-4
Acts 26:12-18

September 12

Monotony Of The Journey

1843

At this point on the Trail, duties could become so repetitous that **monotony** would prevail. John Boardman described it this way: " . . . a person is thinking of the tedious and tiresome journey . . . As soon as camp is struck, then get wood, make fire, cook and eat, then mend pants, moccasins, pack-saddles, . . . Then comes making bed, and by that time , one only thinks of enjoying respose . . ." **89**

Today

Do you get in a rut with your daily **routine**? You arise, go to work, come home, watch TV and go to sleep. On Saturdays you "putter" around the house and yard. On Sundays you go to church, go out to eat, rest, do chores and get ready for another week. Each week seems the same. How can you break this routine, and add more variety, spice and meaning in your life?

Lesson On Finding Meaning In Life

Solomon tried it **all**. He accumulated wealth, completed massive building projects, acquired knowledge, worked hard and indulged in many pleasures. At the end of his life he declared, "Meaningless! Meaningless! . . . Everything is meaningless." His final conclusion to find meaning was to "**Fear God** and keep His commandments, for this is the whole duty of man."(Ecclesiastes 12: 8,13) How does God want you to vary your life's schedule?

Related Passages: 1 Kings 4:26-34; Job 28
Rom 11:33-36

September 13

Three Island Crossing

1843

At Three Island Crossing the emigrants decided to cross the Snake River to the north side. William Newby recounts "that they drove their wagons 100 yards across the stream to the first island and then about 75 yards more to the second. From the second island they had to chain the wagons **together** to make the final crossing . . . about 900 (total) yards. By working together, most wagons made it across without incident. One independent person, Miles Eyers, tried to cross himself, and lost his life and mules. **90**

Today

Do you try to figure something out yourself, or do you rely on the collective judgment of a group? Are you an introvert, prefering much solitude, or an extrovert, enjoying the companionship of others? Remember John Dunn's famous quote, "No man is an island."

Lesson On Fellowship

The disciple John relates an intimate relationship with Christ to **fellowshipping** with Christians. "If we claim to have fellowship with Him yet walk in the darkness, we lie and do not live by the truth. But if we walk in the light, as He is in the light, we have fellowship with one another, and the Blood of Jesus, his Son, purifies us from all sin."(I John 1:7) How's your relationship quotient?

Related Passages: Prov 27:6; John 15
James 4:1-6

September 14

Trading With The Indians

1843

At this point of the journey, many emigrants were running short of **provisions**. Fortunately, they could trade some of their clothing for a more basic essential-dried salmon caught by the Snake Indians. Fremont comments on the oddly-dressed Indians: "We now very frequently saw Indians . . . very many of them were oddly and partially dressed in over-coat, shirt, waistcoat, or pantaloons, or whatever article of clothing they had been able to procure in trade from the emigrants . . ." **91**

Today

Today if we want an item, we **exchange** some of the money we have earned for the right to purchase a commodity. Bartering and trading are not used as frequently as in the pioneer days. How do you determine what of value you will give up to get something else in return?

Lesson On What To Trade

Jim Elloitt, a martyred missionary, insightfully stated, "A man is no fool who gives up what he cannot keep to gain what he cannot lose." Paul similarly states, ". . . I consider everything a loss compared to the surpassing greatness of knowing Christ Jesus my Lord, for whose sake I have lost all things. I consider them rubbish, that I may gain Christ."(Philippians 3:8) Have you made this exchange?

Related Passages: John 11; Rom 5:6-11
1 Pet 2:18-25

September 15

Fragrance Of The Desert

1843

The terrain of the Snake River plain was overgrown with sweet-smelling three-foot **sagebrush.** This hardy plant made travel difficult, so the emigrants "alternated the five or six leading wagons every few miles to spread the toil of breaking down and crushing the coarse stubble under the feet of the oxen and wheels of their wagons." **92** Nevertheless, the pioneers must have enjoyed the strong aroma of this "staple of the desert."

Today

How important are **fragrant smells** to you? Do you grow flowers, not only for their visual beauty, but their aromatic qualities? Do you have apple, cherry or dogwood trees that blossom in the Spring, spreading their sweet fragances throughout the yard? Do you take time to literally smell the flowers?

Lesson On Fragances

Paul uses the metaphor of smell to characterize the fruitful Christian. ". . . God, who always leads us in triumphal procession in Christ and through us spreads everywhere the **fragrance** of the knowledge of Him. For we are to God the **aroma** of Christ among those who are being saved and those who are perishing. To the one we are the smell of death; to the other the **fragrance** of life . . ."(2 Corintians 2: 14-16) Are you a "fragrant" Christian?

Related Passages: Gen 8:20-21; Lev 1:7-9
John 12:1-8; Phil 4:14-20

September 16

Baptism In The Snake River

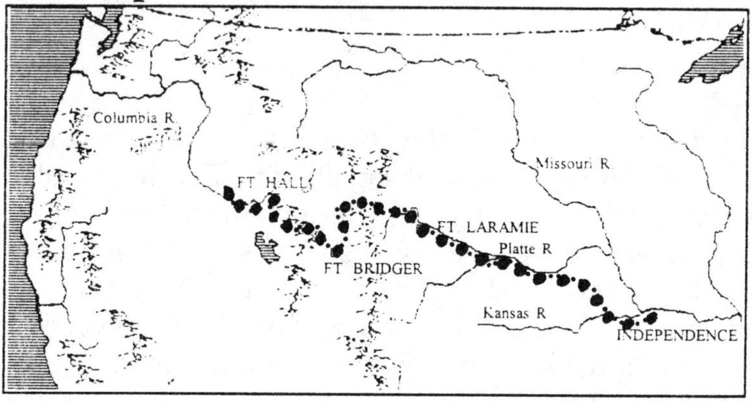

1843

During a Sunday Service, or as a result of one pioneer sharing his or her faith with another, someone probably prayed to ask Jesus Christ into their life. This **personal commitment** may have been done privately. However, this new Christian would have wanted to make this commitment **public.** With a minister, and the nearby waters of the Snake River, a meaningful baptism could be arranged.

Today

Have you been baptized? Was it as an infant or as an adult? Were you sprinkled or immersed in water? Jesus teaches in the Gospel of Mark that baptism is **not** correlated with eternal life, but is a symbolic act of obedience after you have made a commitment to Christ. He promised, "Whoever believes and is **baptized** will be saved, but whoever does not believe(does not say 'and is not **baptized'**) will be condemned."(16:16) Jesus does not equate baptism with salvation. The important step is that you have received Christ, and He is directing your life. You may later choose baptism as an act of obedience.

Related Passages: John 3; Col 2:11-15
1 Pet 3:18-22

Week Eighteen: September 17-23

Ft. Boise

This week the Oregon Emigrating Company reached Ft. Boise, **fourth fort** on their journey. They had now traveled over 1,500 miles since leaving Independence four months ago.

September 17

"Tired, cranky and impatient"

1843

Some of the roughest terrain of the journey lie 274 miles between Fort Hall and Fort Boise, in Southern Idaho. There was little water or grass, and their provisions were dwindling. The men were **tired, cranky** and **impatient**. **93**

Today

Have you had many consecutive "bad hair days." Everything is getting to you-the kids, job, neighbors, even the neighbor's dog, who keeps barking at night, causing you to become more tired. How do you regain your strength to cope with life's daily problems?

Lesson On Regaining Strength

God promises that "those who hope in the Lord will **renew** their strength. They will soar on wings of eagles; they will run and not be weary, they will walk and not be faint."(Isaiah 40:31) Are your soaring like an eagle, or struggling on the ground?

Related Passages: Nahum 1:7; Ps 138:7
Rom 8:28; 2 Cor 4:8-9

September 18

Embittered By The Journey

1843

Because of many adverse circumstances over seventeen weeks, some emigrants "hit the wall," or "saw the elephant." They may have second guessed why they started to Oregon in the first place. Since it was too late to turn around, they may have protected themselves from further hurts by becoming **bitter** and cursing their sorry situation.

Today

How do you cope with **adverse circumstances**? Do you blame someone else for your problems, even when you chose a certain path. Do you ask God, "Why me?" Do you become bitter and resentful that these seeming setbacks are happening to you? What can be done to prevent you from reacting to your situations with a negative attitude?

Lesson On Bitterness and Resentfulness

Solomon and Paul knew human nature. Solomon says, "Each heart knows its own **bitterness**, and no one else can share its joy."(Proverbs 14:10) Paul, describes our human nature: "Their mouths are full of cursing and **bitterness**."(Romans 3:14) Paul commands us to, "Get **rid** of all **bitterness** . . . (and to) be kind and compassionate to one another, forgiving each other, just as Christ forgave you."(Ephesians 4:31-32) Christ's power can truly melt away your wrath and bitterness.

Related Passages: 1 Sam 1:9-11; Prov 5:3-6
2 Cor 1:3-4; Eph 4:25-32

September 19

Nomadic Travelers

1843

The Oregon Emigrating Company could be considered **nomads** during their journey to Oregon. These pioneers "were members of a group of people who had no fixed home and moved or migrated from place to place." **94** Even though the emigrants' goal was to eventually own and occupy a permanent house or farm in Oregon, they had no home on the way. Every day they had a new "address" on the plains. But they were migrating with a **purpose.**

Today

Our modern day nomads are the **homeless** people. They wander our streets, asking for food or money. You see their signs along the road, "Homeless, hungry, need help," "Will work for food," "Stranded with a family." Need gas money." How do you react to these poor-looking people? Do you ignore them, or give them monetary assistance? How do you know their signs are depicting reality for them?

Lesson On Nomads

Jesus sounded like a nomad when he stated, "Foxes have holes and birds of the air have nests, but the Son of Man has no place to lay his head."(Matthew 8:20) Exodus records the Israelites' wandering forty years in the desert before they reached their "promised land" in Canaan. It's not necessarily bad to be a nomad, **if God is directing** your **wanderings.**

Related Passages: Josh 1; Ruth 1; Ezra 8:31-36
Matt 2:13-15

September 20

Desert Plants

1843

Even though the desert is dry and not conducive to lush greenery, a large variety of plants grow in this harsh environment. Some of the 400 adaptive species include sagebrush, rabbit brush, crested wheatgrass, wire lettuce, desert parsley, syringa, bitterbush and possibly wild **mustard,** which grows into a large dark yellow plant. **95**

Today

What is your impression of the desert? Do you see it as only brown, treeless, dry and lifeless, or as a place where a variety of plants and animals live in a unique **ecosystem**? Some people like the desert for its change of colors, its spaciousness, cool nights, bright stars and its ability to sprout flowers after a rare rain. It takes faith and imagination to visualize the beauty of the desert blooming.

Lesson From The Mustard Seed

Jesus used the example of the mustard plant to illustrate the importance of faith: "Because you have so little faith . . . if you have faith as small as a **mustard seed,** you can say to this mountain, 'Move from here to there' and it will move. Nothing will be impossible for you."(Matthew 17:20-21) Here Jesus is saying that, even with your little faith, you will be able to accomplish **great things for God.** Do you have this depth of faith?

Related Passages: Mark 11:22-24; Rom 10:17
Heb 11:1-6; James 5:14-15

September 21

Equinox On The Trail

1843

The pioneers experienced the **fall equinox** at Ft. Boise. On this, the first day of autumn, the length of day and night were approximately the same. Shorter days meant they would have to arise in the dark. More of their evening activities would also be without daylight. The days would continue to become shorter, and the nights longer, as they drew closer to their goal of Western Oregon.

Today

How do you adapt to the change from longer to shorter days, with their continual longer nights? Do you curtail your outdoor activities, such as picnics and fishing, to spend more time indoors reading and watching TV? Do you look forward to the days gradually lengthening again after the winter solstice? Over the course of the year, the daylight and nighttime hours are **balanced.** How do you balance your life's activities?

Lesson On The Balanced Life

Jesus personified the balanced life. In Luke 2:52 we read that He "grew in wisdom(**intellectual**) and stature(**physical**), and in favor with God(**spiritual)** and men"(**social**). Jesus took time to communicate with His Father, to learn, to take care of His body, and to spend time with others. Are you living the four parts of the balanced life?

Related Passages: Ex 23:25-26; Deut 10:12; Josh 24:15
Rom 12:10-13

September 22

Birds In The Desert

1843

Along with the variety of plants and animals in the desert the pioneers probably saw some of the following **birds**: tanagers, with their brightly colored plumage; kestrels, a small falcon; the mountain bluebird, the state bird of Idaho; the brown rock wren; the northern harrier hawk; and the large brown and white great horned owl. **96**

Today

What kinds of birds do you have in your yard? You may have bright red cardinals, orange-breasted robins, brown sparrows or the caw of the black crow. If you live in the country, the soothing sound of the yellow meadowlark, or the brash magpies and bluejays, may be heard. These birds were created by God for our enjoyment. How important are they to you?

Lesson About The Sparrow

Jesus uses the example of the **sparrow** to illustrate how important humans are. "Are not two sparrows sold for a penny? Yet not one of them will fall to the ground apart from the will of your Father. And even the hairs on your head are numbered. So don't be afraid; you are worth more than many sparrows."(Matthew10:29-31) Since His eye is even on the common sparrow, how much more will He watch over us? After all, we are created in the image of God.(Genesis 1:27)

Related Passages: Gen 1:20-23; 7:13-16; Ps 124:6-8
Luke 12:22-28; Acts10:9-16

September 23

Reflecting At Farewell Bend

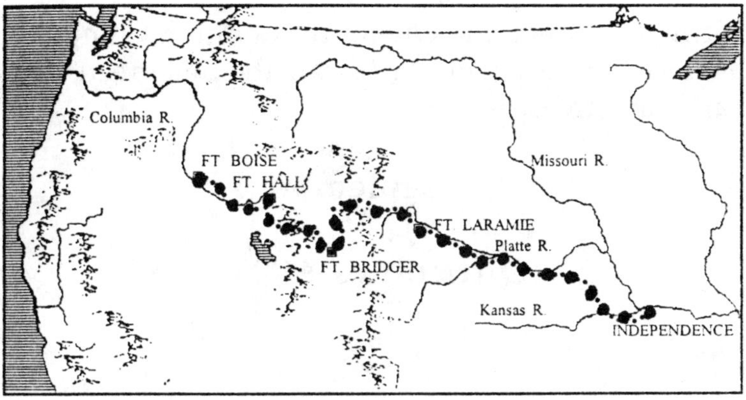

1843

The emigrants had been following the Snake River, their lifeline for 330 miles across present-day Idaho. Since the river curved north, and they needed to continue west, the pioneers departed the river for good at **Farewell Bend**, on the present-day Oregon border.

Today

Farewell greetings are usually difficult, especially for departing family and close friends you may not see for some time. I Thessalonians 5: 16-17 describes a dramatic event called the **rapture**, with no time to say good-byes: "For the Lord Himself will come down from heaven, with a loud command, with the voice of the archangel and with the trumpet call of God, and the dead in Christ will rise first. After that, we who are still alive and are left will be **caught up** together with them in the clouds to meet the Lord in the air. And so we will be with the Lord forever." Will you be leaving the earth then with other "born-again" believers to be with your Lord forever? That will be a happy farewell!

Related Passages: Luke 9:57-62; 2 Cor 13:11-14
Rev 19:6-10

The Burnt River Canyon

During this week the Oregon Emigrating Company left the sagebrush desert behind and saw the first green valleys with many pine trees.

September 24

Difficulties At The End

1843

"In one of the cruel ironies of the Oregon trail, the most difficult stretches occured when the emigrants were least prepared to handle them." **97** If the Trail had run **west** to **east**, that is, from Oregon eastward to Missouri, the difficult Columbia River, Blue Mountains, Burnt River Canyon and the Snake River Plateau would have been traversed while the pioneers were still fresh and had adequate provisions. Instead this part of the Trail remained to **test their stamina** to the end.

Today

How many times have you experienced **difficulties** right before achieving a goal? It may be the final exam before receiving course credit. How about the pain of childbirth right before your child is delivered? Or running the last lap of a race?

Lesson On Coping With Difficulties

"God is our **refuge** and **strength**, an ever-present help in trouble."(Psalm 46:1) We only need to call on Him in our difficulties.

Related Passages: Psalm 27:1-14; 37:23; 138:7

September 25

Teamwork Needed

1843

The small Burnt River cut through a ravine with steep sides and much timber. Jim Nesmith called this canyon, "the roughest country I ever saw." William Newby called it, "the worst road we hav had." For the first time the emigrants had to use double, or even eight or nine yoke of oxen, to pull one wagon up the steep canyon. **98 Cooperation** was needed.

Today

Have you noticed how individuals who do not know each other **cooperate** during an emergency or natural disaster? During a flood volunteers respond to the sandbagging call. People send money to aid earthquake victims in another country. Farmers, particularly the Amish, assist with the harvest if a neighbor is incapacitated. Can you implement teamwork and a shared workload without waiting for a crisis?

Lesson On Teamwork

In I Corintians 12 Paul sees the Church(all Christians) as a "body (that) is a unit, though it is made up of many parts; and though all its parts are many, they form one body.(v12) There are different kinds of service, but the same Lord."(vv4-5) Thus each Christian has a gift to contribute to the Church team. What are your gift(s), and how are you using them to benefit the Body of Christ?

Related Passages: Is 40:26; Rom 8:12, 38-39
1 Cor 12, 14; Jude 24,25

September 26

A Little Bit Of Heaven!

1843

As Peter Burnett left the Burnt River Canyon, he was awe-struck by the next **panorama:** ". . . ranges of tall mountains, covered on the sides with magnificent forests of pine, the mountain tops being dressed in a robe of pure snow, and around their summits the dense masses of black clouds wreathed themselves in fanciful shapes, the sun glancing through open spaces upon the gleaming mountains. . ." **99**

Today

What is the most beautiful **natural scenery** you have witnessed? Was it snow-capped, rugged high mountains? Maybe you saw the sun setting across the ocean, with its glittering light dancing across the waves. Whatever it was, it can't compare to **heaven.**

Lesson On The Awesomeness Of Heaven

The Book of Revelation provides a glimpse of the **new heaven** and earth, and the **holy city,** the new Jerusalem. John decribes it as shining "with the glory of God, and its brillance was like that of a very precious jewel, like the jasper, clear as crystal. It had a great, high wall with twelve gates, and with twelve angels at the gates."(21:11-12) A river of life flows "from the throne of God and of the Lamb down the middle of the great street of the city."(22:1-2) Is this your heavenly city?

Related Passages: Ps 11:4-7; Acts 2:14-21
Heb 9:11-15; 11:13-16

September 27

Marking Flagstaff Hill

1843

After 1,600 miles of mainly brown and dusty desert, the emigrants finally left Virtue Flat and descended Flagstaff Hill into the **Powder River Valley**. In the distance they saw the magnificent tree-covered Blue Mountains of Oregon . This view boosted their spirits, but gradually the realization set in that they would have to **cross** the same mountains they were enjoying.

Today

Today the Flagstaff Hill Monument, an eighteen-foot high pillar of cemented cobblestones, marks the path of the pioneers over this hill. The view is still beautiful, with the green irrigated Baker Valley below. How important are **monuments** in marking significant events in a person's life?

Lesson On Making Monuments

Genesis 28:10-15 records Jacob's dream at Bethel. In it he saw angels on a staircase, and the Lord promising to give "you and your descendants the land on which you are lying."(v 13) After awakening Jacob exclaimed, "How awesome is this place! This is none other than the house of God; this is the gate of heaven. Early the next morning Jacob took the stone he had placed under his head and set it up as a **pillar** . . (vv17-18) Is there a place where God spoke to you, and you would like to make a pillar of remembrance?

Related Passages: Josh 24:25-28; Job19:21-27
Ps27:4-6; Is 28:16-19

September 28

Peaceful Powder River Valley

1843

The emigrants' first view of the Powder River Valley must have evoked an **idyllic peaceful scene**. Overton Johnson describes the valley this way: " . . . we find the hills and Mountains covered with Pines, and the little valleys along the Creeks and Rivers with excellent grass. This valley is about ten miles wide and thirty miles long, a large portion of which has a good soil. It is encircled by hills and Mountains." **100**

Today

What is your idea of a **peaceful scene**? Is it a "Norman Rockwell painting" depicting a rural setting, with contented cows grazing on the green grass? Or is it a picture of a thundering waterfall crashing on the rocks far below. If you look closer you will see a bird in a nest, safely tucked on a ledge behind the waterfall. Can you have peace in the middle of turmoil?

Lesson On Peace

Jesus promised us His peace, regardless of our circumstances. In John 16:33 He states, "I have told you these things, so that in Me you may have **peace**. In this world you will have trouble. But take heart! I have overcome the world." "For God is not a God of disorder but of **peace**."(I Corintians 14:33) Do you have the peace of God in your situation?

Related Passages: Is 26:3,12; John 14:27
Phil 4:6-9

September 29

The Lone Pine

1843

For decades a large **solitary pine tree** had been a landmark for travelers throughout the plain. Peter Burnett looked for this magnificent tree, only to find it was gone. He recounts, "I was perplexed for a moment to know whether I was going the right direction. . . . That **brave old pine**, which had withstood the storms and snows of centuries, had fallen at last by the vandal hands of man." **101**

Today

Joyce Kilmer personalizes the aesthetic beauty of a **tree** in his classic poem:

> "I think that I shall never see
> A poem as lovely as a tree.
> A tree whose hungry mouth is prest
> Against the earth's sweet-flowing breast;
> A tree that looks at God all day,
> And lifts her leafy arms to pray;
> A tree that may in Summer wear
> A nest of robins in her hair;
> Upon whose bosom snow has lain;
> Who intimately lives with rain.
> Poems are made by fools like me,
> But only God can make a tree." **102**

Lesson On The Value Of Trees

The Psalmist sees the godly as flourish(ing) "like palm trees, and grow(ing) tall as the cedar of Lebanon."(Psalm 92:12) Are you a flourishing **tree**?

Related Passages: Gen 2:8-14; Job 14:7-10
Ps 1:3; Prov 3:17-18

September 30

Reflecting On Stewardship

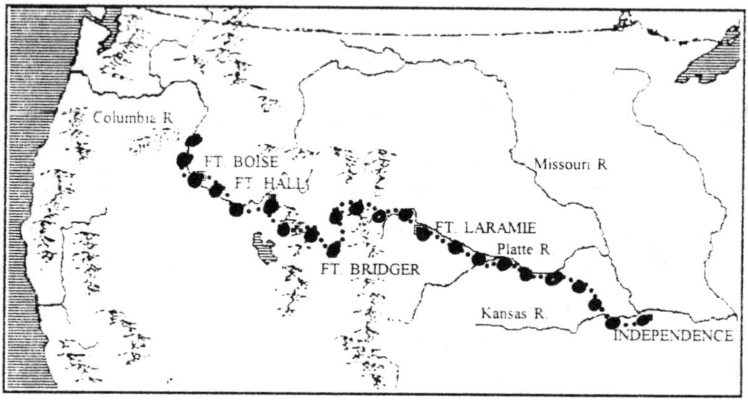

1843

The cutting down of the lone pine by one of their own members highlighted the problem of **responsible stewardship** of the earth's natural resources. This person was only thinking of his immediate need for wood, and not the other benefits this tree held-as a landmark, shade and aesthetic beauty. These pioneers had no reforestation plan for future settlers. Are we better stewards of our environment today?

Today

Today we have "clear cutting" of our pine trees, combined with restoration projects. However, we have more types of pollution today than during the pioneer days. Witness the belching of smoke from factories, the dumping of toxins and pesticides in our lakes and rivers, the littering of highways and the carbon monoxide from our automobiles. David says, "The earth is the Lord's, and everything in it."(Psalm 24:1) Isaiah says, ". . . the whole earth is full of His glory."(6:3) What are you doing to **restore** and heal God's glory to the earth?

Related Passages: Ps 37:34; Matt 25:34
Eph3: 6; 2 Pet 1:4

The Blue Mountain Crossing

The emigrants had worried about crossing the high Rocky Mountains until they traversed South Pass, an easy opening for them. They didn't realize the most **difficult mountains** to cross were the "**Blues.**"

October 1

Uncertainty Of Life

1843

Today the emigrants lost another person, a Mrs. Ruby. She was buried in what Peter Burnett described as, "one of the most beautiful valleys in the world , embosomed among the Blue Mountains, which are covered with magnificent pines." **103**

Today

Do you have your whole life **planned** out, doing only what you want to do? What if something-like your **death**-would interrupt these plans? Would you be ready to die?

Lesson On The Uncertainty of Life

James cautions us against making our own plans: "Why, you do not even know what will happen tomorrow. What is your life? You are a mist that appears for a little while and then vanishes."(4:14) If we have the Son, we have **eternal life.**(I John 5:12) What kinds of plans have you made? Whose plans are they?

Related Passages: 1 Kings 2:2-3; Rom. 12:1-2
1 John 5:11-13

October 2

Fertile Fields

1843

The Grand Ronde Valley, with "land to delight the farmer," gave the pioneers a glimpse of their "**promised land**," the Willamette Valley. In fact some emigrants liked it so much they seriously thought of settling there. Ninevah Ford said, "there was a parley with the emigrants as to whether we had better stop there or not. It was a beautiful country. They would have stopped and colonized it if we had had provisions." **104**

Today

You don't have to be a farmer to appreciate green **fertile fields** with crops of corn, beans, or potatoes. The green signifies life coming from the God-given nutrients found in the soil, together with adequate moisture and sunshine. In what grain fields are you working?

Lesson On Working In Fertile Fields

Jesus says we should be working in His field, harvesting souls for the Kingdom of God. "Do you not say, 'Four months more and then the harvest'? I tell you, open your eyes and look at the **fields!** They are ripe for **harvest.** Even now the reaper draws his wages, even now he harvests the crop for eternal life, so that the sower and reaper may be glad together. Thus the saying 'One sows and the other reaps' is true."(John 4:35-37) Are you sowing and reaping souls for eternal life?

Related Passages: Ps 126:5-6; Prov 22:8
2 Cor 9:6-15; Gal 6:6-10

October 3

Blazing A Trail

1843

The same pine trees that the pioneers enjoyed from a distance had to be cut down to make a trail for the wagons. This was the first time on the journey that a **path** had to be literally blazed. Ninevah Ford stated, "We camped many times in sight of our former night's camp. We found it very laborious and very hard cutting that Tamarisk timber with our dull axes that we had not ground since we left Missouri." **105**

Today

Have you ever "**cut a new trail**" for yourself? Perhaps it was creating a new job or ministry for yourself. You wondered if you could actually do this new task. From where did you obtain the resolve for your mission?

Lesson On Finding God's Will

Moses had a literal **blazing experience** with God at the burning bush. Even though God commanded Moses to ". . . go. I am sending you to Pharoah to bring my people the Israelites out of Egypt,"(Exodus 3:10) Moses was still hesitant, and made excuses for not being qualified to accomplish God's mission. Through a series of miraculous signs, as recorded in Exodus 3-4, Moses finally realized God was with him to accomplish His will. Have you had a "**burning bush**" experience with God, confirming His mission for you?

Related Passages: 1 Chron 22:13; 1 Kings 2:2-3
Prov 16:3; Rev 3:20

October 4

Slothful Pioneers

1843

Blazing a trail through the "Blues" was slow and tough going. Not every man shared this laborious task equally. According to Ninevah Ford, "It devolved on some 40 persons to make that road. The lazy ones dropped back, not for the purpose of screening themselves, but to rest their cattle, so they stated, but we imputed it to their diffidence in regard to the work." **106**

Today

What type of **occupation** do you prefer-an entrepreneurial business, where you are usually rewarded for your hard work, or a profession such as teaching, where every instructor receives the same salary, if they possess similar education and years of experience? The former type of work is more risky, since your business can fail, while the latter type is more secure. Thus the **tradeoff.** What does the Bible say about how hard we should work, or what our purpose in life should be?

Lesson On Work

Solomon sees the **value of hard work**: "Lazy hands make a man poor, but diligent hands bring wealth."(Proverbs 10:4) Paul warns against idleness: "If a man will not work, he shall not eat."(2 Thessalonians 3:10) Christians work primarily for God, and not their employer. For whom are you working?

Related Passages: Deut 8:18; Josh 1:8
Is 48:17; 3 John 2

October 5

Confidence In An Indian Guide

1843

Marcus Whitman had been guiding the emigrants since Fort Hall. When Dr. Whitman was urgently called back to his mission, he assigned a faithful Cayuse Indian named Stickus to lead the pioneers across the "Blues." The **confidence** the emigrants had in Stickus was expressed by Ford, "wherever he directed us to go, there we went, without searching for any other route."

Today

In what types of institutions or persons do you have **confidence**? Is it in our political system, and its leaders? How about your boss at work? Your minister at church? The teachers at school? Your friends and neighbors? Your own family members? In whom can you really place your unwavering trust?

Lesson On Confidence

Solomon sees the Lord as our **security.**(Proverbs 3:26) Jeremiah sees those "who (trust) in the Lord, whose **confidence** is in Him," as being blessed.(17:7) In Hebrews we are encouraged to "approach the throne of grace with **confidence,** so that we may receive mercy and find grace in our time of need."(4:16) I John says we have **confidence** in receiving what we ask God, if we ask according to His will.(5:14) Is your security only in God?

Related Passages: Is 40:26; John 10:27-29
Rom 8:38-39; Phil 1:6

October 6

Snowstorm In The "Blues"

1843

It took the emigrants four tough days to cross the Blue Mountains. On the third day they were surprised with a **snowstorm.** Although not serious, this storm served as a reminder that winter was setting in-and they still had approximately 300 miles to go! **107**

Today

Is your "**snow glass**" half full or half empty? On the postive side, do you enjoy its pure white color, and the chance to hear it crunch as you "step on it" for skiing or snowshoeing? Or on the negative side, do you think of snow as a hindrance, preventing you from driving or making more work with shoveling? Are snowstorms cozy(if you're inside) or scary(if you're stranded)? How does winter affect you?

Lesson About Snow

Snow is used as a metaphor for **purity** and **cleanliness**. The Psalmist asks God to, "Cleanse me with hyssop, and I will be clean; wash me, and I will be whiter than **snow**."(Psalm 51:7) In Isaiah God promises the Israelites that even "Though your sins are like scarlet, they shall be whiter than **snow**; . . " (1:18) When you see the snow covering the ground, you can be reminded that, "If we confess our sins, He is faithful and just and will forgive us our sins and **purify** us from all unrighteousness."(I John 1:9)

Related Passages: Is 55:10-11; Dan 7:9-10
Matt 28:1-8; Rev 1:12-18

October 7

Celebrating Sunday Communion

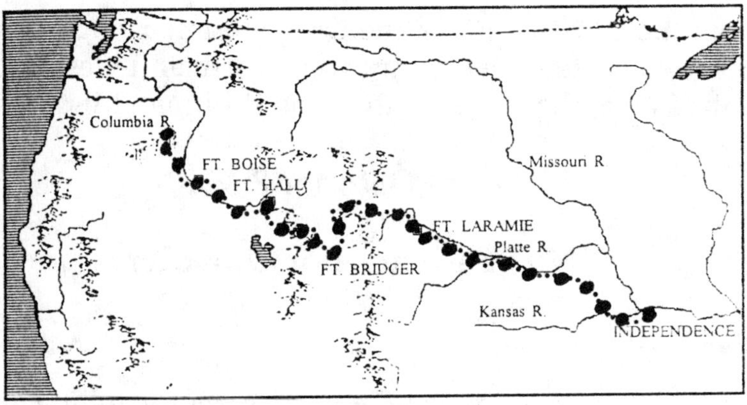

1843

While camping in the Powder River Valley, the pioneers may have participated in a sacrament that had been used in their home churches. A communion service could be held in the open area. They had bread, or juice, and possibly wine, symbols of Christ's body and blood, respectively, for this observance, which remembers what Christ did for us on the cross.

Today

How serious are you when you participate in the **Lord's Supper**? Paul warns us that "A man ought to examine himself before he eats of the bread and drinks of the cup. For anyone who eats and drinks without recognizing the body of the Lord eats and drinks judgment on himself. That is why many among you are weak and sick, and a number of you have fallen asleep."(I Corinthians 11:28-30) **Communion** is an excellent time to ask God's forgiveness while meditating on what Christ did for you. Thank God for the gift of His Son!

Related Passages: I Cor 10:14-17; 2 Cor 6:14-16; 13:14

Week Twenty-One: October 8-14

The Whitman Mission

From the Umatilla River, the Oregon Emigrating Company took two routes. One group went north and west to Fort Walla Walla, the other north to the Whitman Mission.

October 8

No "Patience For Dawdlers"

1843

During this week of traveling over gently rolling hills between the Umatilla and Walla Walla Rivers, the wagons spread out and traveled at their own speed. With 200 miles left, those in front "no longer had any **patience** for dawdlers." **108**

Today

How much patience do you have for someone who is slower than you in some aspect? What about a student in class that needs an answer repeated, while you, who have understood it the first time, have to wait? What about someone who can't keep up with you physically? How can you **cultivate** patience?

Lesson On Patience

Paul encourages us to be **patient**.(Ephesians 4:2) If we are filled with the Holy Spirit, we will be **patient**, one of the Fruits of the Spirit.(Galatians 5:22) Do you have the sweet spirit of patience?

Related Passages: Prov 19:11; 25:15
2 Cor 1:3-7; 2 Pet 3:8-9

October 9

Converting The Cayuse Indians

1843

Marcus and Narcissa Whitman established their mission with the Cayuse in 1836. They found their **converts** few, and the work difficult. These Indians accepted the teaching of the Christian Gospel, but continued to practice their old native ways. Marcus had to personally travel to St. Louis in 1842 to convince the Presbyterian Missionary Board to continue their support, which they did until 1847. **109**

Today

Have you tried to live a Godly life with your family, friends, neighbors, or co-workers? At some point have you then told them when you accepted Christ, and how His power enables you to lead a Christian life? Maybe they were not receptive to your **testimony.** What can you now do to try to win them to Christ?

Lesson On Witnessing

Christians are promised the Holy Spirit to witness to others. "But you will receive power when the Holy Spirit comes on you; and you will be My **witnesses** in Jerusalem, and in all Judea and Samaria, and to the ends of the earth."(Acts 1:8) We are "not(to be) ashamed of the gospel, because it is the power of God for the salvation of everyone who believes . . ."(Romans 1:16) Do you rely on His **power** to witness to others?

Related Passages: Prov 12:17; Matt 18:15-20
John 1:8

October 10

The Kindness of Dr. Whitman

1843

Dr. Whitman had promised provisions to those families desparately in need of food. John McClane found a fair trade at the mission: "(Dr. Whitman) furnished the emigration with fat beef. . . He furnished them with fat steers . . . the finest beef I ever saw. He furnished one of these big steers for two head of our cattle. If persons had not anything to trade with he would let them have the meat anyhow. He was one of those men who would divide the last thing he had." **110**

Today

Do you know people that are **kind** and **generous**? These people go out of their way to assist and please others, without expecting anything in return. They prefer to work "behind the scenes," making others look good, without receiving credit. How can you be more kindly to others?

Lesson On Kindness

Kindness is a Fruit of the Spirit. Proverbs states, "A **kind-hearted** woman gains respect. . ."(11:16), "A **kind** man benefits himself . . ."(11:17) and ". . . blessed is he who is **kind** to the needy."(14:21) Paul encourages us to "Be **kind** and compassionate to one another . . ."(Ephesians 4:32) and ". . . always try to be **kind** to each other and everyone else."(I Thessalonians 5:15) What is your level of kindness?

Related Passages: Dan 4:27; 1 Cor 13
2 Tim 2:22-26

October 11

The Love of The Whitmans

1843

Your July 8th devotional in this book pertained to the martyrs' deaths of Marcus and Narcissa Whitman, and eleven others, at the hands of the Cayuse Indians on November 29,1847. The Whitman's demonstrated their **love** to these Indians for eleven years at the mission. Because of a tragic misunderstanding over a measles epidemic, their ministry came to an end.

Today

For whom would you be willing to sacrifice your life? Would you run into a busy street to save your child from being hit by an automobile? Would you be willing to die for our nation during warfare? Would you risk your life to pull a stranger from a burning building? How far does your love commitment go?

Lesson On Love

Jesus' love for us went all the way to the cross. "This is how we know what **love** is: Jesus Christ laid down His life for us. And we ought to lay down our lives for our brothers."(I John 3:16) "Greater **love** has no one than this, that He lay down His life for His friends."(John 15:13) Since **love** is a Fruit of the Holy Spirit, we can use this power to love one another ". . . since God so loved us, we also ought to **love** one another."(I John 4:11) Can you love the **lovely** and **unlovely** as well?

Related Passages: Ex 15:13; Deut 5:8-10
2 Chron 5:13-14

October 12

Having A Gentle Spirit

1843

One historian described the Great Migration of 1843 as "composed of people of pronounced character, rudely arrogant and aggressive rather than tame and submissive." **111** The meek stayed home and never ventured on the Trail. More pioneers with a gentle spirit would have been helpful to ameliorate some of the disputes that erupted after almost six months of the journey.

Today

Do you possess a "Type A" personality- achievement-oriented, hard-driving and easily stressed? Or are you relationally-oriented, laid-back, and not easily upset-characteristics of a "Type B" personality? A **gentle spirit** would be more typical of the latter personality type. How can a "Type A" person become a gentle spirit in dealing with others?

Lesson On Gentleness

Jesus possessed "**meekness** and **gentleness**."(2 Corinthian10:1) **Gentleness** is a Fruit of the Spirit.(Galatians 5:23) Through this power, we can "let (our) **gentleness** be evident to all."(Philippians 4:5) "Always be prepared to give an answer to everyone who asks you to give the reason for the hope that you have. But do this with **gentleness** and **respect**."(I Peter 3:15) Do you witness to others with a gentle spirit?

Related Passages: 1 Cor 4:14-21; 2 Cor 10:1-6
1 Tim 6:11-16

October 13

Importance Of Prayer

1843

Those pioneers who traveled to Fort Walla Walla, in today's Southern Washington, were the first to see the "Great River of the West"-the Columbia. It was an awesome sight! Fremont describes the river as "a noble object, and has here attained its full magnitude." **112** This was a good time for the emigrants to offer a prayer of thanksgiving to God for protecting them on the overland portion of the journey.

Today

How often, and under what circumstances, do you pray? Do you pray only at specified times(meals or bedtime) or throughout the day? Do you pray only when a crisis develops, or to thank God for your daily blessings as well?

Lesson On Effective Praying

James states that "The **prayer** of a righteous man is powerful and effective."(5:16) Paul commands us to "**pray** continually."(I Thessalonians 5:17) We should always be in an attitude of prayer, ready to ask God for His power in our lives. The acronymn ACTS will assist you in focusing your prayers:

Adoration-praising God for who He is
Confession-asking for God's forgiveness
Thanksgiving-for God's working in our lives
Supplication-asking for specific requests

Have you learned the secret of releasing God's power through prayer?

Related Passages: Is 65:24; Matt 21:22
Heb 4:16

October 14

Singing Hymns Of Praise

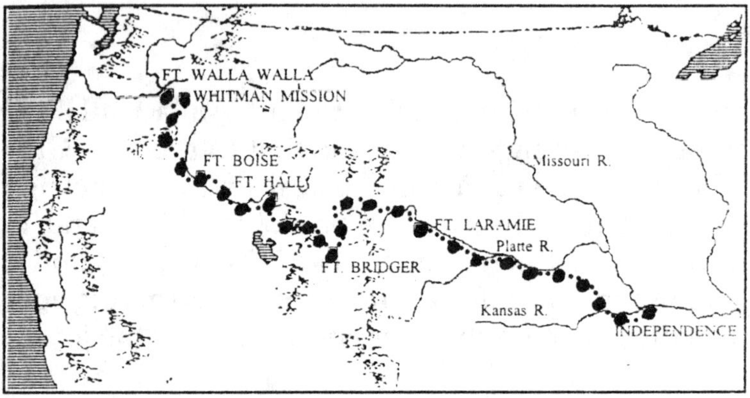

1843

The emigrants undoubtedly camped along the steep banks of the wide Columbia River, the border between present-day Oregon and Washington. As part of their Sunday Church Service, they may have sung hymns of praise and deliverance. With approximately 200 miles to go, some would face their most difficult challenge on this mighty river.

Today

Some of the hymns they may have sung, which we still do today, include the following titles: "Abide With Me;" "How Great Thou Art;" "It Is Well With My Soul;" "Great Is Thy Faithfulness;" "A Mighty Fortress Is Our God;" "Blessed Assurance;" "Holy, Holy, Holy;" and "Amazing Grace." Modern praise songs are used in contemporary worship services. Some of these titles include: "The River Is Here;" "Lord I Lift Your Name On High;" "Majesty;" "We Exalt Thee;" "Give Thanks;" and "To Him Who Sits On The Throne." "Sing for joy to God our strength."(Psalm 81:1) Praise His Name for singing!

Related Passages: Ps 147:1; 43:1; Eph 5:18-20
Heb 13:15

The Columbia River Indians

Most of the pioneers' encounters with the Indians were friendly. However, the Columbia River Indians had seen too many whites, and they took advantage of them through robbery.

October 15

Uncleanliness

1843

Fremont described these Indians as ". . . **disagreeably dirty** in their habits. Their huts are crowded with half-naked women and children, and the atmosphere within anything but pleasant to persons who had just been riding in the fresh morning air." **113**

Today

Do you despise persons who are dirty, disheveled and smell badly? They may be a homeless person or an addict? Do you think "cleanliness is next to Godliness?"

Lesson On Being Clean

Jesus saw the Pharisees for who they were: "You **clean** the outside of the cup and dish, but inside they are full of greed and self-indulgence. Blind Pharisee! First **clean** the inside of the cup and dish, and then the outside will also be **clean.**"(Matthew 23: 25-26) Are you clean where it counts-inside?

Related Passages: 1 Kings 3:10-14; 2 Cor 7:1
Heb 9:13-15; 1 John 1:9

October 16

Building Boats For The Storms

1843

At Fort Walla Walla, some emigrants had prepared for floating down the Columbia by building boats. Fremont saw ". . . a considerable body of emigrants, under the direction of Mr. Applegate, . . . had nearly completed the building of a number of Mackinaw **boats**, in which they proposed to continue their further voyage down the Columbia." **114**

Today

Have you ever been in a boat during a **storm** at sea, or on a deep river or lake? It's a helpless feeling, knowing your small craft is subject to the swells and rhythms of the waves. Where is your security during the "storms" of life?

Lesson On The "Storms" Of Life

When "they cried out to the Lord in their distress . . He **stilled the storm** to a whisper; the waves of the sea were hushed."(107:28-29) Jesus and His disciples were on a boat about to be swamped by a storm. "The disciples went and woke Him, saying, 'Master, Master, we're going to drown!' He got up and rebuked the wind and the raging waters; the **storm subsided**, and all was calm. 'Where is your faith?' He asked His disciples."(Luke 8:24-25) Do you have faith Jesus will calm your "storms?"

Related Passages: Nah 1:2-3; Matt 9:1-8
Mark 4:35-41; Luke 5:1-3

October 17

The Inspiring Cascade Mountains

1843

When John Arthur saw the **Cascade Mountains**, and Oregon's tallest peak **Mt. Hood**, bathed in snow at 11,239 feet high, he concluded; "owing to the lateness of the season, it was thought unwise for the emigrating party to undertake to make a wagon road over the **Cascade Mountains**, lest the way might be blockaded with snow and women and children perish with cold and hunger." **115** They would have to travel the rest of the way by treacherous water.

Today

Do mountains possess a **spiritual dimension** for you? Do they draw you closer to God? Are you inspired by seeing them, or standing on the summit, enjoying the vistas?

Lesson On A "Mountaintop Experience"

Mark 9:2-8 records how, on a high mountain, Jesus "was transfigured before them. His clothes became dazzling white . . ."(v 2-3). After seeing Elijah and Moses with Jesus, Peter exclaimed, "Rabbi, it is good for us to be here."(v 5) We, like Peter, may want to **remain on the mountain**. But as Oswald Chambers observes, we were not made for mountaintop experiences alone. "We see His glory on the mountain, but we never live for His glory there." **116** Have you experienced the "mountaintops" in your walk with God?

Related Passages: Nah 1:15; Ezek 34:11-16
Is 55:12-13

October 18

Going Down Into The Valley

1843

The pioneers were headed to the fertile Willamette Valley. Along the way they traveled through the Platte River and Bear River Valleys. This mostly level terrain was the easiest over which to travel. Even if the emigrants climbed some of the higher landmarks along the way(Courthouse and Jail Rocks, Scottsbluff or Independence Rock), they eventually had to come **down to the valley** to continue their journey.

Today

After climbing a mountain, do you come down refreshed, ready to tackle the **daily tasks** of living in the valley? Or would you rather stay on the summit, being inspired by the views and solitude?

Lesson On Living In The Valley

Even Jesus and His disciples came down from the Mount of Transfiguration.(Mark 9:9) According to Chambers, "The true test of our spiritual life is in exhibiting the power to descend from the mountain. . . We are not made for the mountains, for sunrises, or for other beautiful attractions in life. . . We are made for the **valley** and the ordinary things of life, and that is where we have to prove our stamina and strength." **117** "Mountaintops are for views and inspiration, but fruit is grown in the **valleys."118** Has your spiritual fruit developed?

Related Passages: Deut 11:8-12; Is 40:3-5
Joel 3:14-16

October 19

The Self-Control Of An Indian Pilot

1843

The most dangerous part of the journey for some was the trip down the Columbia River to Fort Vancouver. Peter Burnett purchased an old boat from the Hudson's Bay Company(HBC) built especially for navigating the Columbia. Many emigrants employed an Indian to pilot their boats, and to navigate the treacherous rapids. Burnett described their guide as "cool, determined, and intrepid." **119**

Today

Have you ever gone white-water rafting in Idaho, which has 3,000 miles of white water-more than any other state? You place your confidence in your guide, who you assume could handle a crisis. How do **you** react in a crisis situation? Are you "cool" and disciplined under pressure, or do you "crack?"

Lesson On Self-Control

Self-control, or restraint, is so important that Paul lists it as a Fruit of the Spirit.(Galatians 5:23) It "is honored by the Lord as the "anchor virtue"(listed last) on His relay team that runs life's race for His glory." **120** Peter sees self-control as important to the Christian. He admonishes us to "be clear minded and **self-controlled** so that you can pray."(I Peter 4:7) **Self-control** is part of a list of admirable traits.(2 Peter 1:6) Do you possess this restraining virtue?

Related Passages: Acts 24:22-27; 1 Cor 7:5-7
1 Pet 1:13-16

October 20

The Goodness of John McLoughlin

1843

Why would the Chief Factor of Fort Vancouver(owned by the British HBC) befriend the American pioneers? William Newby recounts the generosity of Dr. John McLoughlin: "Arriving at the Cascades,(the emigrants) found that the generous Dr. Loughlin had sent up batteaux to take the party to Fort Vancouver. . . Food and fuel, and every needed supply were furnished . . . and not a cent was charged for all that trouble and splendid treatment . . ." **121**

Today

Do you know persons who are **generous** with their time and money, expecting nothing in return? They may not share any interests with you, other than their desire to be good to you. You naturally wonder what they're up to or ask "What do you want?" Their altruism baffles you, but you know it is **real**. Jesus was that way.

Lesson On Goodness

Many references refer to God's goodness. "He is **good** . . ."(2 Chronicles 7:3) The Psalms challenges us to "Taste and see that the Lord is **good**,"(34:8) ". . . for your Name is **good**," (52:9) and ". . .You are **good** and forgiving."(86:5) Jesus acknowledges that "No one is **good**-except God alone(Mark 10:18) We can be good only through Christ in us.

Related Passages: Ps 100:4-5; 119:68
Matt 19:11-17

October 21

Reflecting On God's Faithfulness

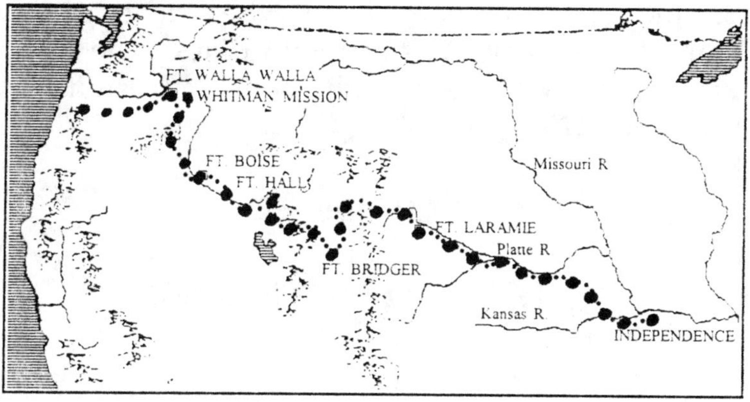

1843

With their arrival at Fort Vancouver, the Oregon Emigrating Company had conquered their **last obstacle**-the rapids at the Cascades on the Columbia. They had traveled 1,900 miles-only thirty miles from their goal-Oregon City! On this last Sunday of their journey, they could now recount their **blessings** and God's **faithfulness** in bringing them safely this far.

Today

Do you take time to meditate on God's faithfulness to you? How has He provided for you, never left you and given you wisdom to make decisions pleasing to Him? He has never broken a promise. He established a covenant with Abraham: "I will make you into a great nation and I will bless you; I will make your name great, and you will be a blessing."(Genesis 12:2) "God pursues a continuing love relationship with you that is **real** and **personal**." **122** He is faithful!

Related Passages: Ps 36:5; Jer 23:28-29
Hosea 2:19-20

Arriving In Oregon

Since the emigrants spread out when floating down the Columbia, they arrived at **different** times. The first person to arrive in the Willamette Valley was Jim Nesmith on October 27, 1843. **123**

October 22

Reflecting On The Fruits

1843

By this time the pioneers were anxious to get settled in their new land. Some of them had brought **seeds** from home, planning to plant them for a bountiful crop the following fall. The fertile Willamette would grow a variety of **fresh fruit** that would be on their own land!

Today

Have you ever thought how God could create the variety of orchards we enjoy? How many different fruits do you grow, buy or eat?

Lesson On The Fruit of the Spirit

When we are filled with the Holy Spirit according to the command in Ephesians 5:18, we receive all the following qualities: **love, joy, peace, patience, kindness, goodness, faithfulness, gentleness, and self-control**. Are you a "Spirit-filled" Christian, possessing these nine qualities?

Related Passages: Matt 7:15-20; 12:33-37
John15; Rev 22:1-5

October 23

From Civilization To Civilization

1843

After the harrowing experiences drifting down the Columbia, the emigrants could finally enjoy the hospitality of John McLoughlin and the amenities of Fort Vancouver. "The emigrants were truly back in civilization. . . Instead of leaving civilization and plunging into a wild unsettled frontier,(and staying there like most pioneer journeys) the Oregon emigrants crossed an untamed wilderness only to return to civilized life." **124** Thus their journey took them through several **stages**-from civilized to uncivilized to civilized life.

Today

Our lives are in stages. We are born, grow up to adulthood, graduate from high school and possibly college, start a career, get married, have children, reach our peak earning years, become grandparents, retire and then die. How can you add **meaning** to these seasons of life?

Lesson On The Stages Of Life

The Psalmist sees "The length of our days is seventy years-or eighty, if we have the strength; yet their span is but trouble and sorrow, for they quickly pass, and we fly away."(90:10) His advice to us: "Teach us to number our days aright, that we may gain a heart of wisdom."(90:12) Are you gaining wisdom with each passing year?

Related Passages: Ps 1:3; Prov 15:23
Gal 6:9; 2 Tim 4:2

October 24

The End Is Near

1843

From Fort Vancouver to Oregon City was only thirty miles. The pioneers could probably smell the fertile Willamette. Yet some of the emigrants were so sick and worn out by the journey that they stayed at the Fort's hospital for medical attention-all for free. **125** Once they left the Fort, they could really concentrate on preparing for their **new life.**

Today

How do you respond to a project that is just about to be completed? Do you **sprint** to the finish line, or barely **limp** over? The authors are excited that this book project, a dream come true, is close to being finished. We have the end in sight!

Lesson On "The End"

Matthew 24, Mark 13, Luke 21 all forecast the signs that will happen before the Christians are "raptured" from the earth(I Thessalonians 5:16-17). These **events** include: wars and rumors of wars, famines, earthquakes, pestilences, signs in the heavens, persecution of Christians, apostasy, appearance of false prophets and wickedness. Jesus predicts, "I tell you the truth, this generation(seeing all the above signs fulfilled) will certainly not pass away until all these things have happened."(Luke 21:32) Many Biblical scholars think all these signs are happening now. Are **you** ready for the end of the world?

Related Passages: John 14:2-3; 2 Thess 1:3-12
2 Pet 3:10-13

October 25

"As Far As The East Is From The West"

1843

Jim Nesmith was the first to arrive in the Willamette Valley! He had left Elm Grove, in the spring(May 22, 1843) and arrived in Oregon City in the fall(October 27). He had traveled 1,932 miles in 158 days, averaging twelve miles per day. Other emigrants would cover the same distance in a longer time. The last one in this party to arrive at Oregon City was Edward Lenox toward the end of November. "It remains as one of the most extraordinary events in recorded history." **126**

Today

What took the pioneers over **five months** of ardous travel, we can now cruise in our cars in **five days.** The distance you travel over the Trail is measured geographically, in miles. However, the distance from the east to the west has another meaning in the Bible.

Lesson On "The Distance Of Forgiveness"

The Psalmist uses the metaphor of **distance** to help us comprehend what Jesus did for us on the **cross.** " . . . as far as the east is from the west, so far has He removed our transgressions from us."(103:12) Thank Him for forgiving us our sins!

Related Passages: Ps 23:3; 37:23; 1 Cor 2:9
Heb 11:16

October 26

Reaching The "Promised Land"

1843

When the Oregon Emigrating Company finally reached Oregon City, there were no friends, relatives, dignitaries nor parades to welcome them to their "**promised land**." You would think they would stage their own celebration-bringing out the wine and hoisting the flag. Here's how one diary entry matter-of-factly read: "Reached Oregon City. Went to work the next day." **127**

Today

Where is your "promised land?" Is it where you plan to retire? Do you look at rankings of the best places to live, and then decide to move there? Or is your **land** where you are living at the present time? How can you make your promised land into a reality?

Lesson On Living In The "Promised Land"

After wandering in the desert for forty years, the Israelites reached their "promised land" over the Jordan River. It was a land filled with milk and honey. In Deuteronomy 28 God promised them prosperity if they would obey His commands.(vv1-14), but curses would come upon them if they disobeyed.(vv 15-68) Elihu reaffirms these promises: "If they obey and serve Him, they will spend the rest of their days in prosperity and their years in contentment."(Job 36:11) Your "**promised land**" can be obeying God right where you are.

Related Passages: Gen 12:7-9; Josh 1:1-9
1 Chron 28:8

October 27

Settling In The Willamette Valley

1843

After reaching Oregon City, the pioneers became settlers, spreading throughout the Valley to build houses and claim land. They would have to endure a cold, rainy winter before they could plant crops in the spring. But their new life in their chosen land had begun! They would begin to make new friends and establish relationships, and maybe never move again! They would talk about their "**Trail Experience**" the rest of their lives.

Today

Are you mainly a **pioneer** or a **settler**? Do you like to take risks and move to new places(pioneer), or would you rather build a nice house and live and work in one place(settler)? What kind of houses should we be building and living in?

Lesson On Building And Living In Houses

David warns, "Unless the Lord builds the **house**, its builders labor in vain."(Psalm 127:1) Jesus compares those who practice His words with those who do not heed His advice, to wise and foolish builders, respectively.(Matthew 7:24-27) Jesus is "preparing a place for (us) . . . and (He) will come back and take (us) to be with (Him) . . ."(John 14:2,3) Soon we "born-again" Christians will live with Him in heaven. Together we will worship our King forever! Welcome home, pioneers!

Related Passages: Ps 127:1; Jer 29:5-7
Matt 16:17-20; Acts 7:49-50

ENDNOTES

1 Lloyd W. Coffman, **Blazing A Wagon Trail To Oregon: A Weekly Chronicle Of The Great Migration Of 1843,** Enterprise, OR, Echo Books, 1993,3.
2 Jay Mennenga, **Lessons From The Pioneers: Reflections Along The Oregon Trail**, Second Printing, Burley, ID, Potential Press, 1995, 26.
3 Ibid., 32.
4 Ibid.
5 Ibid, 33.
6 Coffman, 25.
7 Ibid., 27.
8 Ibid., 31-32.
9 Ibid., maps on the first page of each week, Week One-Week Twenty-two
10 Mennenga, 46.
11 Ibid., 56.
12 Coffman, 35.
13 Ibid.
14 Mennenga, 78.
15 Coffman, 42.
16 Ibid.
17 Ibid., 41.
18 Ibid., 42.
19 Ruis, David, "Mercy Is Falling," Mercy Publishing, 1995, 1996 Men's Retreat, 36, song.
20 Coffman, 29.
21 Ibid.
22 Ibid., 44,46.
23 Ibid., 56.
24 Ibid.
25 Mennenga, 39.
26 **Women's Study Bible**, Nashville, TN, Thomas Nelson Publishers, 1569,1572.
27 Mennenga, 78.
28 Coffman, 58.
29 Ibid.,

30 Ibid., 61.
31 Mennenga, 160.
32 Coffman, 70.
33 Mennenga, 35.
34 Ibid., 78.
35 Coffman, 71-72.
36 Ibid., 76.
37 **The Overland Migrations**, Washington, D.C., Division of Publications, National Park Service, US Department of the Interior, 85.
38 Mennenga, 14.
39 Coffman, 78-79.
40 Mennenga, 87-88.
41 Coffman, 80.
42 Ibid., 81.
43 Mennenga, 98-99.
44 Ibid., 68-69.
45 Coffman, 87-88.
46 Mennenga, 127.
47 Coffman, 88.
48 Ibid.
49 John D. Unruh, Jr., **The Plains Across**, Chicago, IL, University of Illinois Press, 1979, 87.
50 Coffman, 89-90.
51 Ibid., 92.
52 Ibid., 93.
53 Ibid., 94.
54 Mennenga, 90.
55 Ibid., 159.
56 Coffman, 98.
57 Ibid., 99.
58 Mennenga, 90.
59 Coffman, 99.
60 Charles R. Swindoll, General Editor, **The Living Insights Study Bible**, Grand Rapids, MI, Zondervan Publishing House, 1996, 625.
61 Coffman, 101.

62 Ibid., 102-3.
63 Ibid., 105.
64 Ibid., 107-8.
65 Ibid., 108.
66 Swindoll, **The Living Insights Study Bible,** 65.
67 Coffman, 108.
68 Ibid., 109.
69 Ibid., 110.
70 Ibid., 113.
71 Ibid.
72 Ibid.
73 Mennenga, 54.
74 Coffman, 120.
75 Ibid., 118.
76 Ibid., 119.
77 Ibid.
78 Ibid., 120.
79 Ibid., 120-121.
80 Ibid., 122.
81 Mennenga, 132.
82 Ibid., 136.
83 Ibid., 138.
84 Ibid., 144-145.
85 Ibid., 146-147.
86 Charles R. Swindoll, **Intimacy With The Almighty**, Dallas, TX, Word Publishing, 1996,43.
87 Coffman, 129.
88 William E. Hill, **The Oregon Trail: Yesterday and Today**, Caldwell, ID, Caxton Printers, Ltd.1987, xxv.
89 Coffman, 130.
90 Ibid., 132-133.
91 Ibid., 131.
92 Ibid., 128.
93 Ibid., 135-136.
94 **The American Heritage Dictionary,** Third Edition, New York, Dell Publishing, 1994, 566.

95 Craters of the Moon National Monument, Idaho, sign, September 18, 1997.
96 Ibid.
97 Coffman, 138.
98 Ibid., 139.
99 Ibid., 140-141.
100 Ibid., 140.
101 Ibid., 141.
102 Mennenga, 85.
103 Coffman, 143.
104 Ibid.
105 Ibid., 144.
106 Ibid., 145.
107 Ibid., 145-146.
108 Ibid., 148.
109 Ibid., 75.
110 Ibid., 150.
111 Ibid., 171.
112 Ibid., 152.
113 Ibid., 156-157.
114 Ibid., 153.
115 Ibid., 157.
116 Oswald Chambers, **My Utmost for His Highest**, Grand Rapids, MI, Discovery House Publishers, 1995, October 2.
117 Ibid, October 1,2.
118 Billy Graham, Billy Graham Evangelistic Association Calendar, 1993, quote.
119 Coffman, 160.
120 Swindoll, **The Living Insights Study Bible**, 1251.
121 Coffman, 167.
122 Henry T. Blackaby and Claude V. King, **Experiencing God: Knowing and Doing The Will of God,** Nashville, TN, Lifeway Press,1990, 20.
123 Coffman, 158.
124 Coffman, 167-168.
125 Ibid., 167.
126 Ibid., 158,168.
127 Mennenga, 168.

BIBLIOGRAPHY

Books

The American Heritage Dictionary, Third Edition, New York, Dell Publishing, 1994.

Blackaby, Henry T, and Claude V. King, **Experiencing God: Knowing and Doing The Will of God**, Nashville, TN, Lifeway Press, 1990.

Chambers, Oswald, **My Utmost for His Highest,** Grand Rapids, MI, Discovery House Publishers, 1995.

Coffman, Lloyd, **Blazing A Wagon Trail To Oregon: A Weekly Chronicle Of The Great Migration Of 1843**, Enterprise, OR, Echo Books, 1993.

Hill, William E., **The Oregon Trail: Yesterday and Today**, Caldwell, ID, Caxton Printers, Ltd., 1987.

Mennenga, Jay, **Lessons From The Pioneers: Reflections Along The Oregon Trail**, Second Printing, Burley, ID, Potential Press, 1995.

The Overland Migrations, Washington, DC, Division of Publications, National Park Service, US Department of the Interior.

Swindoll, Charles R., **Intimacy With The Almighty**, Dallas, TX, Word Publishing, 1996.

Swindoll, Charles R., **The Living Insights Study Bible,** Grand Rapids, MI, Zondervan Publishing House, 1996.

Unruh, John D. Jr., **The Plains Across,** Chicago, IL, University of Illinois Press, 1979.

Women's Study Bible, Nashville, TN, Thomas Nelson Publishers.

Other Sources

Craters of the Moon National Monument, Idaho, sign.

Graham, Billy, Billy Graham Evangelistic Association Calendar, 1993, quote.

Ruis, David, "Mercy Is Falling," Mercy Publishing, 1995, 1996 Men's Retreat, 36,song.

Did You Enjoy Reading This Book?

Do You Have Questions Of The Authors?

Contact Them At:

Potential Press
PO 272
Pocatello, ID 83204-0272
208-232-3825
208-232-2771(fax)
1-888-232-3820(toll-free)
e-mail backbeyond@gemstate.net

Reflections

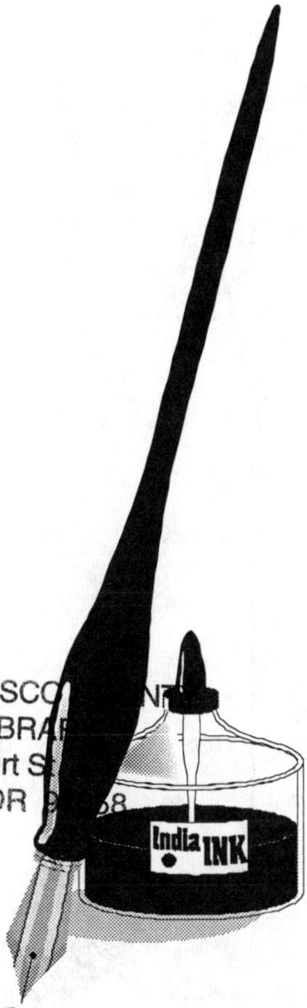

Reflections